Lies to Light

BRANDY SEIGNEUR

ISBN 979-8-89130-200-6 (paperback)
ISBN 979-8-89130-201-3 (digital)

Copyright © 2024 by Brandy Seigneur

All rights reserved. No part of this publication may be reproduced, distributed, or transmitted in any form or by any means, including photocopying, recording, or other electronic or mechanical methods without the prior written permission of the publisher. For permission requests, solicit the publisher via the address below.

Christian Faith Publishing
832 Park Avenue
Meadville, PA 16335
www.christianfaithpublishing.com

Printed in the United States of America

January 23, 2019

As I sit here typing these words, I am reminded of the many excuses I have thought or spoken as to why I cannot write a book:

1. I talk like a hillbilly.
2. I'm a mother to a very busy toddler.
3. I don't know who would read it or where to even start.

A short time later, I realized that these are all lies from my enemy, Satan—someone I once knew much better than my Savior.

God had put it in my heart a few different times over the past five years to write a book, yet these excuses have kept me from even trying. So here goes nothing.

My prayer is that my story inspires someone and that they too can feel the overwhelming peace and grace from God.

Contents

Chapter 1: Young Love 1
Chapter 2: Protector Named Grandpa 4
Chapter 3: Life Questions 8
Chapter 4: Imagination 11
Chapter 5: Locked Away 14
Chapter 6: Unwanted/Unloved 18
Chapter 7: Breaking Free 21
Chapter 8: Deserted Once More 24
Chapter 9: New Beginnings 27
Chapter 10: Satan's Fiery 31
Chapter 11: Two Become One 34
Chapter 12: The Call 38
Chapter 13: Amazing Grace 41
Chapter 14: Endo 45
Chapter 15: Accepted Sinner 49
Chapter 16: Expected Guest 52
Chapter 17: Fertility Baggage 55
Chapter 18: For This Child I Prayed 59
Chapter 19: God's Grace 62
Chapter 20: Little Miracle 66
Chapter 21: Guarded Heart 71
Chapter 22: Introducing Mommy 75
Chapter 23: Foundation of Christ 78
Chapter 24: It's O-fish-al! 81
Chapter 25: Roar! 84
Chapter 26: God's Incredible Love 89

CHAPTER 1

Young Love

My life began thirty-five years ago when I was knitted in my young mother's womb.

My mother—weighing about one hundred pounds with dark curly hair—lived at home with my grandma, grandpa, and her two brothers, including one who was born mentally challenged.

Grandma had told me stories about the birth of her son who was born with this condition. She explained that it was an extremely challenging pregnancy. She told me that during his birth, the cord connecting the two of them became wrapped around his neck, putting both her life and his at risk. They both survived, but it left my uncle with a lifelong mental disability.

This uncle is my grandparents' eldest child, followed by the birth of my mom and her younger brother.

Grandpa had three children from a previous marriage. I never really saw any of them growing up as they lived in different parts of the country.

My mother was fourteen years old when she met my father, a strongly built guy with wavy light brown hair who was fifteen years old. They began a sexual relationship resulting in my mother becoming pregnant at such a young age.

This pregnancy was a secret my mother held deep within her until I was just about to be born. My mother told me that she dressed in bigger shirts and sweatshirts to mask her pregnancy from my grandparents and other family members.

She explained that she didn't know what was going on in her body or why it was growing, but she knew all she wished was that it would go away.

She would sneak my father into her bedroom window at night as they continued a sexual relationship.

My father stole from my grandparents' home on multiple occasions, oftentimes taking money or household items. Mom had never portrayed him to be a very nice guy.

My family did not approve of their toxic relationship. My grandparents knew about my dad and didn't like him or his family. My dad's father was abusive to his wife as alcohol played a big role in his life. My father was repeating the behavior that he had witnessed growing up.

At approximately eight months pregnant, my mother complained of stomach pain. She and my grandma were driven to the doctor as Grandma never had the desire to have her driver's license. As my grandmother sat in the waiting room, I often wonder if she ever suspected anything concerning my mother. She was very busy with her disabled son, who required much of her energy and attention.

My mother walked out of the room and into the waiting room, where my grandma was sitting. As they looked at each other, my grandma asked my mom, "Well, what did they say?"

My mother, scared and afraid of her response, spoke the words "I'm pregnant."

Grandma couldn't believe what she was hearing and quickly realized they had about two weeks to prepare for a baby in her home.

My mother had to deliver this news to her father. My grandpa was heartbroken. He was on the road much of the time as a truck driver for different companies. He became angry at the thought of the man who stole from him and slept with his baby girl, as she had been a "daddy's girl." My grandpa told my mom and grandma to leave the house and to raise "that baby" (me) somewhere else. He wanted no part of raising a baby created by a man he didn't like. My grandma told me that she put her foot down and told Grandpa that they were not going anywhere.

A few weeks after my family heard about my mother's pregnancy, I was born. In May of 1983, a baby was born: an eight-pound, nine-ounce baby girl with straight dark hair and a perfect little body. My mother had just turned fifteen years old only one month prior. She left the hospital with my grandma and me.

I will forever be grateful that, although scared and confused, my mother chose life.

CHAPTER 2

Protector Named Grandpa

At their home, my grandparents had set up a crib in my mother's bedroom and made it very clear that she would care for her baby, not them. My mom told me that I was a very good baby and that I only cried if I needed something. She said that one night, I cried, and before she could get out of bed to care for me, my grandpa walked into her darkened bedroom and picked me up from the crib.

My mother was scared as she thought, *What are they going to do to my baby?* These were her thoughts as she knew Grandpa still wasn't happy with her about being pregnant. He was very disappointed in her.

As my mom got up from bed, she quietly walked down the hall and peeked into my grandparents' room. I'm sure fear was surrounding her as to what her eyes would see. She slightly opened the door to get a better look, and there I was, lying happily between my grandma and grandpa. They were talking to me and laughing as I made noises and smiled back at them. My mother told me that from that day forward, I was wrapped around Grandpa's finger, and he loved me dearly. It showed. My grandpa was always so kind to me and showed me how much he loved me.

He took walks with me around the block, and he took me to recycle with him to cash in our aluminum cans. Grandpa took me everywhere with him. He even purchased me a shirt at a truck stop that read "My daddy is a trucker." I suppose he couldn't find one that said *grandpa*, so it would suffice. It became one of my favorite shirts as a child, and I wore it until it no longer fit.

My grandpa had told my mother that my father was not welcome in his home. I was his little girl now, and nothing or no one would come between us.

My parents had a destructive relationship that soon ended following my birth. Because of this, I never established an ongoing healthy relationship with my mother or father.

One story my grandma told me about my dad was that I, at the age of two, helped solve a crime that my dad had committed. She said that while playing in my playpen in the living room of her home, I saw something. Grandpa's wallet came up missing. While my mom and grandparents gathered in the living room to talk about it, I kept saying "dada" while pointing to the back door of the house just past the kitchen.

Through questioning my mom, my grandparents were sure I had seen my dad come into their home and steal my grandpa's wallet. To my grandparents, this was why I was pointing at the door while repeating my father's name.

My dad spent time in jail for many crimes before going to prison. He was in prison most of my life. My mother continued to pursue happiness wherever she thought it would be found. Mom birthed five children by four different men, and we are all two years apart in age.

My dad had ten children by eight different women, resulting in me being the oldest of fifteen children. Most of my dad's children, I do not know. Over the years, I've received messages from strangers who noticed that we looked alike, only to find out we have the same dad.

My mother was always looking for acceptance in men. She wanted to feel loved and appreciated but instead had multiple failed relationships and marriages. It was during this time that I spent much of my childhood at my grandparents' house. Mom, being so young, allowed my grandparents to care for her four children, adding a fifth child two years later. My grandma, who was short and plump, did the cooking and caring for all of us kids. We were never hungry, and we knew that at Grandma and Grandpa's house, we were always safe. Oftentimes, Grandpa, tall and skinny, would take his baseball bat or gun outside to run off my mom's abusive ex-boyfriends or ex-husbands.

We knew no bad men would get to us with Grandpa around. He was our protector, and we loved being in their home. My grandparents lived in an old run-down house with chipped yellow paint, which was across the street from a junkyard. The house often smelled like cigarettes and vanilla air freshener. The view from Grandma's little porch, where she loved to sit, was a metal junkyard with cars stacked ten high, all smashed together.

There was a fence separating the junkyard from the street, and just behind the junkyard, there was a train track. Trains traveled down those tracks multiple times a day.

It was usually loud from big crane engines or a train blowing its horn as it went by. Grandma loved being outdoors, and at night, she would invite my siblings and me to her porch. The light from a large junkyard tower was bright red, and it was always flashing across the sky. Grandma had a passion for anything sci-fi and told us that the red light from the junkyard was a UFO. We would scream and run into my grandpa's bed, where he lay comfortably. Suddenly, his comfy bed had four others in it: my siblings and me. He yelled at Grandma for scaring us as we all laughed, knowing better.

We loved our grandma's room, and it's where she and Grandpa spent a lot of their time together. It was always ice-cold as they ran the window air-conditioning unit all day every day. My siblings and I crawled in the down comforter, sometimes resulting in feathers in our hair from the bedding. Grandpa always had a baseball game on. He enjoyed watching the Reds play baseball, and I took this time to nap.

Grandma's home was extremely cluttered as she kept every newspaper, form, and receipt and even loved ones' possessions (those who had passed away). Some things we viewed as trash, but to Grandma, it all meant something special. Especially her recipe book. Grandma loved to cook, and Grandpa made the best biscuits and homemade gravy!

To return the favor, one day, my siblings and I cooked up some delicious snacks for my grandparents to enjoy. This consisted of a ball of bread, minus the crust, covered in peanut butter and loaded with sugar. We delivered this to my grandparents on a beautiful platter, along with our version of homemade coffee.

Although this had to taste horrible and the coffee had to be so watered down and cold, they never let us know it. They spoke to us as if they loved our creation. I'm almost positive that when we left the room to make more, they spit it out.

CHAPTER 3

Life Questions

The memories of Grandma and Grandpa were always good as they made us feel safe, and I had the impression that we also helped them feel complete.

One example of how my siblings and I felt their home became a safe haven happened during a violent storm. During storms, Grandma directed my siblings and me to hide in her fully stuffed closet with her so we were safe. My siblings and I knew they adored us as they watched us grow up while still raising their three kids the best way they could.

Despite the choices my mother and uncles made, my grandma and grandpa still loved them.

One of my uncles was quite the ladies' man, and he often traveled to stay with my aunt and uncle in their Florida home. I had a close relationship with him, and he rarely told me no. He always played games with me and made me feel loved.

One night, while I was sleeping with my grandma in her big bed, I was awakened by a loud noise coming from the kitchen. I slowly crept out of bed, and I quietly walked down the long hallway wearing Grandpa's white shirt, which was hanging down to my ankles. My uncle and his friend were at the kitchen table, eating doughnuts and drinking coffee. From my perspective as a child, his friend was a very tough-looking dark man with a cross earring in one ear. My uncle had many friends, and oftentimes, I would ask to tag along with them.

On one occasion, I asked my uncle, as he was walking out the front door, if I could go with him on a car ride. He told me, "Not this time." I began to cry as he had never told me no. Grandma heard me from her bedroom as I stood at the front screen door with tears pouring down my cheek, and she carried me back to her bed.

On one of the nights when my uncle went out with friends, he was drinking alcohol in his car and was in a horrible car accident. He was thrown so far from the accident site that paramedics didn't know he was lying lifeless in the road for quite some time. After many tests and multiple hospital stays, he was pronounced brain-dead. I no longer had that fun uncle whom I had such a good relationship with prior to his accident. I always had respect for him as my uncle since he was another man besides my grandpa who I felt loved by. It would take the majority of my life to find out from a family member that he was actually the driver of the car containing three more of his friends. He was the one who was drinking and driving before hitting another vehicle. Learning of this information made me feel confused as to why he would drink and drive, although it didn't change how I cared for him later on. He was put into a brain trauma center many miles away from my grandparents home. He was paralyzed and would be wheelchair bound and treated poorly by many staff members over his lifetime with illness and infection attacking his body often. When we would visit my uncle, I was always the last one to enter the room.

My family would all walk in and say, "Oh wait. We have a surprise for you!" Then I would run into the room where my uncle was and give him the biggest bear hug I could! His Christian music was always filling the room. He told my siblings and me that he was going to start his own community and to save all the pens and markers and papers we could. In his mind, the women or girls (including me) were going to be teachers in his community.

These visits were only a few times a year, but we enjoyed his company, and we knew he appreciated us spending time with him. My uncle had a love for birds. I remember helping him care for one at my grandma's home, in the living room. Maybe this is why I now love birds.

CHAPTER 4

Imagination

Family began to mean so much to me, and I thrived on the time they spent with me. My parents were not always present, but my grandparents always let me know I was welcomed. Both of my grandmothers and grandpa did their best to make my childhood enjoyable. My dad's mother tried to make things entertaining. I best remember her as an Indian-looking woman with long black hair and tan skin. She hosted Easter egg hunts for me and my cousins. We would play at their home or at the park across the street.

A vivid memory I recall was when I was about the age of three. I would sit on the pool table in the bar of my grandpa's (dad's dad) home. I rolled all the pool balls into the holes until one of the drunk men talking around the table would retrieve the balls so I could drop them in again and again. The house always smelled like beer and bacon grease.

At the age of seven, I visited my dad in the home of his mother (my grandmother). As I sat on the dark stained carpet with my dad, playing cards and drinking juice, my dad drank his beer. My mother called during this visitation, to talk to me on the phone. When she asked me what Daddy was drinking, I had no idea that in telling her "beer," that would mean I would be taken from him and my grandma forever. Mom had told him to not have any alcohol in my vicinity. Quickly placed in the back of a cop car, I clung to the window screaming "Daddy!"

What did I do? Why was my daddy gone? Why was my grandma gone? Why did I tell Mom that Dad was drinking a beer? This was all my fault.

Due to his alcohol addiction, I no longer had visitation with my dad or my grandma. I was spending much of my childhood at my mother's parents' house. My siblings and I played at their house with our huge imaginations. The apple tree out back became a lovely sheeted home with a cooler of refrigerated food from the house or garden. Grandma's old Avon perfume bottles became secret hidden treasures we buried in the dirt.

On one occasion, I used one of the kitchen knives to cut a hole in the wall of a bedroom, large enough to push a sweeper hose through it. On the other side of the wall was a closet full of Grandma's old smoke-stained clothing. My siblings and I ran the sweeper hose through the hole and called that room the bank. I put that dirty sweeper hose up to my mouth and asked, "May I help you?"

While playing school, I insisted on being the teacher as I was the oldest, creating grade cards for my grandparents to sign. The piano bench became an office desk to a clerk who organized the "bills due." Envelopes became mailboxes taped to the wall, with our names written on them. Pretend play was a big part of my childhood.

My siblings and I created money consisting of lined paper, often written on with Grandma's "winning" lottery numbers. Grandma sure loved her lottery and her plain dark coffee, claiming that one day, she would win millions and own a mansion.

Grandpa was a truck driver, and he traveled often. He loved taking his grandkids on truck drives. We enjoyed napping in his truck, and one time, we thought Grandpa had actually driven us to Florida in his semitruck by accident. Through lots of laughter, he told us that he had just driven us around the block. I was always learning new things as a child. Grandpa taught me to ride my first bike.

He would say, "You ready?" And off I went, hearing his change jingle in his pocket as he jogged, holding tightly on to my seat before letting go. Once, he even let me drive his Oldsmobile car in the yard. Grandma watched reluctantly from her back porch as her ten-year-old granddaughter drove the wheels of that car right over her roses that were planted in nice straight rows. I thought Grandma was going to kill me and Grandpa!

Grandpa would drive me to Willies market, and we would purchase five grab bags filled with penny candy. Me and my siblings would set up our "stores," and we traded candy. Grandpa played and got all the Milk Duds since none of us cared for them.

In the hot summer, Grandma stood in the front yard of her home wearing only her nightgown, and she would sell the tomatoes and other vegetables from her garden to people driving by. Grandma put her money in a mason jar for a rainy day.

Grandpa bought the biggest watermelon he could find, and the barbecues were endless in the summer. Extended family, along with neighbors, joined our backyard gatherings. I remember, at times, Grandpa hired a clown to entertain us and my uncle, twisting balloons into all kinds of animals!

Summertime at Grandma and Grandpa's was full of fun as we played with cousins and neighborhood kids! Days spent with Grandma and Grandpa never got boring.

This beautiful life I had as a child would soon change my life forever.

CHAPTER 5

Locked Away

On Sunday mornings, I would wake my siblings up, dress the girls in one of our three dresses, and wait for the church bus that picked us up out front of Grandma and Grandpa's home. I became a helper, serving cookies and juice on the church bus. I was being given "jobs" and was quickly growing up from a child to a young adult.

Things seemed good to me considering Mom was figuring out her life, spending much of my childhood with men that seemed to be interested in her but not us. Not the five children she gave birth to. How I witnessed this was with my brother being beaten black and blue—or, as I often saw, black and purple. He was always so skinny that you could see his bones.

One event that has never left my memory happened when he was about ten years old, and I was twelve. My stepdad sent my mother and four of her children to get ice cream, excluding my brother. My heart pounded as we left the home, not knowing if he would even be alive when we returned. The anger in my mom's husband was a stronghold. My siblings and I ate our ice cream with Mom. Once we returned home, I stepped into the kitchen, and I noticed my brother standing there with tears pouring down his face.

"Get back in your room!" yelled my stepdad.

That was when I noticed his worst beating yet. From his neck to his ankles, my brother was purple. Welts and bloody stripes covered him. I felt helpless and afraid for him. My heart sank as I saw my little brother quiver in fear of this monster who hurt him. I couldn't understand why we were made to live this life of abuse, especially my baby brother. The abuse continued as he was made to dress as a girl with pigtails since he once played Barbies with my sister and me.

He was forced out of our home at the young and helpless age of ten years old. As I peeked out from under the sheet hung in the only air-conditioned space (the dining room), I noticed two police officers and my brother standing there, talking. They were asking my mom and her husband if they would like for them to scare him by placing him in a cop car or taking him to his dad. They then told the officers to take him to his dad. Now I was losing my little brother! His father was an alcoholic, and they were leaving my brother to live life in the streets at a very young age. Years went by before reconnecting with him. The abuse didn't stop when my brother was removed from the home.

I was locked in my bedroom for months at a time, only to come out to go to the bathroom or to clean the kitchen mess after dinner. My dinner was usually brought to me by one of my siblings. I was excluded from family boating trips and other fun activities, only to sit in my bedroom alone. I had been given a restroom schedule created by my mom's husband (my youngest brother's dad). If the family left the house, he would put a piece of tape on the outside of my bedroom door. When he returned home, if the tape was pulled off, I was beaten horribly for leaving my bedroom. This became extremely difficult when I began my menstrual cycle. At times, I cried in so much pain, waiting to use the restroom until I was told to. I thought that if my grandpa knew of this abuse, he would have done something about it, but we were threatened by Mom's husband to not say a word. To him, what happened in our home stayed in our home. It wasn't anyone's business.

While locked in my bedroom, one day I complained that the intense heat from outside was causing me to black out. My windows were shut as there was no air-conditioning upstairs.

A wet cloth was thrown into my room, and I was told I would be fine.

You may be wondering what I did to deserve this horrible treatment from my mother and her husband. Well, I was asking myself the same question. All I came up with was it's because I got Cs on my grade cards. Not to mention, they really hated my biological father. My sisters were honor roll students, and because I got Cs, they assumed I must be too into boys to focus on my schoolwork. So, to be assured this wasn't the case, Mom took me to get a haircut that was very short so boys wouldn't look at me. They thought that the more they made me look like a boy, the more I wouldn't receive any attention from them.

I felt like my mom had a sense of pity for me but was too suffocated by the feeling of being trapped. She always let men degrade her and manipulate her. They were always telling her what to do or how long to be gone from the home. It is my belief that she was so drawn into this torment that she felt like there was no escape. Oftentimes, my mother would beat me at my stepdad's demand. She'd tell me to scream loud as if it hurt but would only hit me lightly.

These circumstances confused my mind even more. I truly felt like a slave girl, stuck in this abuse of torment. Most of my clothing came from thrift stores, unlike my sister's name-brand clothing. I knew this was not a normal teenage life. My clothes were titled Monday to Friday on the tags so that I wouldn't have a "favorite" outfit and wear it often. I hated my life, and my siblings began to see me as the girl who was locked in her room as they just wanted to please my mother and stepfather. I began to feel like they were beginning to despise me the same way my parents did. My mom spanked me with my pants and underwear down until the age of seventeen.

Left with no self-esteem, I had horrible eye contact when communicating with others and was feeling extremely unloved. I was only allowed out of my bedroom to go to school and church.

One day, I wrote a book on the homemade paper I made in art class. My book was bound with string, and its outside was a papier-mâché material. The story was about an orphan girl who was abandoned and not loved. This book was special to me because it was how I felt—not loved and alone. My stepdad found my book and told me he was going to burn it in a fire outside. I can only assume that he thought his behavior would be caught by someone who might find the book.

I was devastated as this was my first book ever written. I continued to write poetry. Stories and drawings were where I felt safe in an unsafe environment.

CHAPTER 6

Unwanted/Unloved

Mom took us five kids to church and made us sit in the second row behind Mrs. Murray—shouting, praising Mrs. Murray. This was a Methodist church with a strong belief that women don't cut their hair or wear makeup or show their elbows or knees. They showed us love by always being welcoming when we came to church no matter our lives, if they even knew how bad it really was.

As a preteen, I remember one Sunday, I was prayed over by many of the women of the church as I felt the strong urge to go up to the altar. I may have gotten saved that day, but I don't recall, although there was a power I felt overcome me. My stepdad stayed home as my mother, siblings, and I went to church—only to come home to a very upset stepfather questioning who left the toothpaste lid off the toothpaste. If no one fessed up, we all got spanked or beaten. Church trips were somewhat of an escape from the hell waiting for us at home. As I mentioned, at church, I helped serve cookies and juice on the bus and enjoyed the people there showing me love.

One guy showed a little too much love. The church bus driver picked him up from his home and along the route to church, and he would touch me as I walked past him. A mentally challenged adult man giving a quick, sudden touch on my breast that, at the age of twelve, was beginning to develop. He would also touch my butt or private area. I kept this to myself and even sat next to him if I noticed one of my sisters walking to sit beside him (so they wouldn't get touched by him). It would take me more than ten years to ever mention this to anyone. At the church, they talked about a guy who loved me—a guy who saw me as perfect. How am I perfect? I'm so broken. The men in my life up to this point, besides my grandpa, were showing me anything *but* God's love.

By the age of twelve, I already had no self-worth or desire to live. My stepfather would call me stupid or tell me I wouldn't be worth anything to anyone, a lowlife whore like my mother.

He joked that my hips were childbearing hips and that they could get a lot of money out of me by selling me to other countries. This abuse was becoming too much to handle. At times, my mother, in a rage, would grab my face, leaving blood-filled scratches on me as well as constant marks on my body from her beatings.

I told school counselors, and my parents would be questioned, but they were wise about putting on our great family persona to everyone they met. I felt stuck.

Grandma and Grandpa were the only people I felt safe with.

My grandpa had a blood clot in his head, and he suddenly passed away at this time in my life. When my parents told me that Grandpa died and we wouldn't be going to his funeral, I cried out a very loud "no!" as they sent me to my room once more and told me to shut up. I was lost. I wasn't wanted. I wasn't loved. Life was so confusing.

Grandpa's death shook my world even more as he was the only father figure in my life. What would happen to Grandma? Their home? My family? Me?

While Grandma moved into her new home (a senior home), my childhood home was burned down. Devastation settled in me. I knew this hell I was living in, I would be living in it for a very long time. I wrote poetry—dark poetry—many times speaking of death. My poetry and my drawings of the yard from my bedroom window were what helped me grab on to some semblance of a "normal life." Summer months were worse because I couldn't go to school, so I spent my days and nights in my bedroom with no air-conditioning.

I listened to Dixie Chicks, Mariah Carey, or LeAnn Rimes cassette tapes. I had daydreams at the age of sixteen of my prince charming putting a ladder up to my window to rescue me. At school, I was made fun of by the other kids or their older siblings. They teased me because I wasn't allowed to go on any school trips and was not a part of their cliques (their groups). I was bullied by older kids, and they teased and pushed me around daily.

I now hated school. Locked in my bedroom and getting spanked often, I became extremely angry. How could my mom love me? My stepdad hated me, so he was making her hate me too. He disliked my biological father, who spent the majority of my life in prison, and it seemed as if it was my fault.

Chapter 7

Breaking Free

My stepdad always had a job for me to do. Yard work or remodeling homes was not just a man's job. I helped sand, paint, put up walls, and many other home remodeling jobs. My stepdad was not the easiest man to work with. I thought maybe he was so mean due to his handicap. He was hit by a drunk driver while on his motorcycle. He ended up with his legs wrapped around a telephone pole, which left him on crutches for the rest of his life. His legs had no strength to move, and he had to physically lift up his legs to adjust them. I guess, in a way, I felt bad for him. Although he treated me and my mom poorly, it didn't overshadow the pity I had for him. This never stopped him from "flipping homes" or remodeling our house.

    His chores were many. My responsibilities included mowing, doing dishes, and taking care of the old man's dogs next door. I would clean up the newspapers that were all over the floors with dog urine and feces; otherwise, I was locked back up in my bedroom. I would constantly question my life. Why me? Where exactly was this good guy I heard of at church? Why wasn't he getting me away from these monsters who called themselves parents?

My low self-esteem, anger, and hatred went as far as taking a wire hanger to begin cutting my wrist with. I just wanted to end it all. This life was no life at all. I bled and became dizzy many times. I never mentioned this to anyone, and I covered it by wearing long sleeves until the cuts healed.

I was now almost eighteen years old, and although I lied to my parents once questioned—yes, I was absolutely counting down the days. Two weeks away from being eighteen years of age, I took clothes in my book bag to my best friend at school. She had parents who informed me that I could live with them if I got a job and respected their home.

On my eighteenth birthday, I left to go to school and never went home again. I left a note under a towel in my room that Mom later found when she decided to finally leave the house as well. The tape player had a Dixie Chicks song ("Ready to Run") on pause for Mom to listen to. Two of her kids had already left willingly or unwillingly at this point, and we knew that "his kid" (the baby) wasn't going anywhere. I know that my departure was hard for my younger sisters. It hurt me to leave them although I felt that they wouldn't receive the abuse my brother and I had experienced. His dad was awarded full custody of him.

Leaving home was a very nerve-racking experience as I struggled for about two years. I always had the thought that if the cops wanted to, they could still make me go back to that house. I was eighteen but felt like I was still about thirteen.

This was also when I felt free. Free from a restroom schedule, spankings, or being locked up. As I began a life of freedom, I thought it would be a good idea to begin taking birth control to prevent any pregnancy as I was only a teenager. I came into contact with the pregnancy center for girls needing information on pregnancy prevention. As I spoke to the woman at the front desk, she said, "Looks here like you were already prescribed birth control three years ago."

I would have been about fifteen years old. Knowing I was not sexually active, I then asked who had ordered this for me. I stood in that office, tears slowly leaving my eyes, as she said my mother's and my stepfather's names. Why did they order birth control for me? I never saw it, so was it placed in my food without me knowing? This brought many questions with little to no answers. Well, now I had to be prescribed birth control for myself as I began a new and freer life. My best friend and her parents welcomed me into their family home.

No longer attending church, the partying I had only heard about had begun in my life. Two weeks after prom, I lost my virginity. I drank often and smoked weed daily.

Somehow, I managed to graduate high school in 2002. I was taking a business and marketing class as well as a graphic communications class since my parents saw no career in cosmetology. It was a career I saw myself performing very well in someday.

Taking classes that my parents chose for me before I left caused me to not have much interest in class at all. I took more interest in the weekend parties. My friends and I drank and smoked every day—multiple times a day with whatever guys would join us.

This resulted in a low self-worth and confusion as to the direction of my life. The "clubs" and ring girl competitions became my teenage life, and many times, I'd end up drunk on a stage with a bikini on or holding a sign or dancing for hot body contests. I had long blond hair and blue eyes. Guys were starting to notice me.

This was something very new for me. Due to being accepted by men, I began living a chaotic life, bouncing from man to man, home to home, and drug to drug. I began getting kitchen tattoos and multiple body piercings. During this time in my life, I began to feel more like an adult, making more adult decisions. I felt like I didn't have any direction from my mother or father.

I felt a huge disconnection from my own mother. I already didn't have a relationship with my father, and now, I felt the pain of separation from the one who birthed me. This hurt me on the inside. The rejection was not easy to bear as a teenage girl.

CHAPTER 8

Deserted Once More

Not feeling accepted by my parents, I thought it would be a good time in my life to meet my dad. To figure this out for myself. The dad I was taken from at the age of seven. The dad my mom spoke so horribly of.

At the age of nineteen, I showed up at the home I remember the cops taking me from as a child. I was escorted by a boyfriend then left alone at the front door. Filled with nerves and shaking hands, I knocked, and I was invited in by his wife, who was only seven years older than me.

Finally, all the questions I ever had concerning him would be answered. What was his favorite color? Did we think alike? Do we look alike? Do we act alike?

When my dad came into the living room, he hugged me and said he was so happy to see me. His wife cooked up a tasty dinner and offered me some. My dad and I sat together on the couch and looked through old photo books. He said he always wrote letters and sent cards, but none ever made it to me. I know from Mom's conversations that he owed thousands of dollars in back child support.

That was why I never received any of his letters. They were hidden from me.

As I sat there looking at photos with him, I became confused. Some of the pictures in the book were pictures of me at Christmas parties and other events that I had no idea he had attended also. Later, I found out that he hired his friends—who were ironically family members to my stepdad—to capture photos of me for him. This seemed odd.

Although I was suspicious of this, I wanted to know my dad. I looked over at the TV commercial of children in other countries who were starving and sick. I really wanted to feel wanted by a parent and to let my dad see exactly what was in my heart. Quietly, I made a comment about the kids, saying, "Those poor kids. I feel so bad for them."

With so much rage, my dad threw his plate of food across the room, and it shattered on the wall, as he yelled negative, racial words at me. Then he kicked me out of his house.

I left my dad's home that night feeling so heartbroken. I cried as I walked down a long dark road to my grandma's home. I was very scared and lonely. I had been deserted once again.

Would I ever be accepted? I began a more destructive life of sex, drugs, alcohol, and carelessness. I didn't care what dangerous situations I put myself in. I didn't care what happened to me. From bad relationships to worse relationships, I began a trail of brokenness and bitterness.

This resulted in two broken engagements. One relationship was approximately seven years. It ended at the realization he was 99.9% father to a child from a previous relationship. I was not in the position to be a mother, even if the child lived in another state. This caused me to break off the relationship. The second engagement was to my childhood friend who had a crush on me all through school. When we became adults and ran into each other again, sparks flew. I thought that since he liked me my entire life, he would definitely treat me well. Besides, he was in the army.

During one leave for work, he called and asked me to marry him and move overseas with him. I had said yes without even thinking. It wasn't long after that I saw his picture in a newspaper. It stated that an army soldier was becoming engaged and showed him in a jewelry store—with another girl! Well, that engagement with me was off, clearly. I began to consider my own path of life since none of my relationships were working out.

At times, I would party with my parents. My mother and her new boyfriends would attend clubs with me and smoke weed, and occasionally, I would have a beer with my dad and his friends. Many times, I felt as if my dad wanted to "show me off," although he didn't raise me. This was a destructive lifestyle for many years of my life.

Bouncing from job to job, I finally knew the great profession for me: being a stripper. I was pretty and skinny, so it seemed like a reasonable, perfect-paying job. Modeling sounded a bit more professional, so I began another new relationship and a modeling career. This consisted of multiple photo shoots and a violent relationship.

CHAPTER 9

New Beginnings

My third engagement was to a man who was an ex-marine. Discharged for bad conduct, he had visitation with his two-year-old daughter, the product of a one-night stand. She spent the weekends with us in our old restored house in a little town.

I was as broken as ever and was mentally and emotionally abused once more. My ex and I didn't respect one another. We called each other horrible names, and we partied at the bars together when we didn't have his daughter. When we had visitation with her, she lived in the chaos and the anger we held within. Although we tried to create a bond between his daughter and my youngest sister on my dad's side since they were the same age, she was still living in our bondage.

After four years of being engaged, our relationship ended with an attack when my ex-fiancé stormed into our bedroom and punched me in the face at a home party. Now this was enough. For years, I had accepted verbal abuse as I heard it my entire life. My stepdad was always calling me names. I thought I could deal with the mental abuse as negativity controlled most of my thoughts. But this physical abuse I wouldn't accept. I had received hair-pulling and pushing, which resulted in hospital visits due to this abuse, but I persisted in staying unless I was physically hit or cheated on. Any other abuse was accepted. One night, I was kicked in my ribs until I fell to the floor in tears, only to go to the hospital and find out I had two bruised ribs.

The story that my family heard me tell was that I tripped over a porch railing, resulting in my pain. I covered the abuse that I saw as a form of "tough love." My mother and stepfather told me that they loved me, but it was shown in an abusive way most times.

That night, as I lay with a sore face from being hit in the cheek, I slept next to my abuser. I put a body pillow between us, and as alcohol tainted his breath, I fell asleep with the intention of leaving in the morning. I witnessed my mother's abuse, and there was no way I was going to follow in her footsteps.

The very next day, when he left for work, I packed up my belongings from that old farmhouse. Funded by cash advances, I left him, his daughter, my cat, my dog, and my home. This was the hardest choice of my life as he had remorse for what he had done. I, however, knew deep down that if he hit me once, he would do it again. I felt betrayed due to the abuse, but I knew we were not meant to be together forever. We were totally toxic for each other.

I called friends to help me move out while he was at work. I had an astonishing strength that made it possible for me to carry my grandma's wooden queen-size bedroom set, as well as a microwave and other household items. I only took what I knew was mine as I wanted no further communication with my abuser. If I wasn't sure if it was mine or his, I left it in the house.

As I went to pull out of the driveway, crying but determined, I was ready to put the car in drive and go. I couldn't! The huge air conditioner was in the front seat, blocking my gear shift. After adjusting the air conditioner, I was finally ready to begin my new life, free from abuse and pain.

I really had no idea where I would go but knew my mother (in her new relationship) disliked my unhealthy relationship. I showed up on my parents' doorstep crying in the rain and holding a suitcase of my belongings. Mom had remarried, and they had what seemed to be something better than anything she ever had up till now. My mom worked full-time at a doctor's office, and my stepdad was a retired firefighter. My stepdad and I had our differences, but we also some similarities. I still smoked, and he used to. So when Mom would leave for work, we smoked our cigarettes in the garage and had conversations about futures, plans, dreams, and God. That same God I heard about before. The one who apparently loves me. The one man who wants what is best for me.

My stepfather helped me come up with a list containing ten goals I had for my life. Number one was "Marry a man who loves God." I thought that in writing this as a dream, I would be treated like the nice God I had heard about. During these conversations, my stepdad helped me to see my worth. He always encouraged me to believe in myself. My mother treated me kindly as well. When I was sick, she took care of me before leaving for work, then my stepdad cared for me. I saw my mom getting treated better than ever before without my parents help I don't know what my life would have been like.

My parents made my living conditions comfortable. If I was going to be out late with friends, I was told to call and let them know—just be respectful.

I was living the party life with friends on the weekends. During the week, I worked my full-time job at a local adult disabilities company. It was a very humbling job. It made me more thankful for the little things in life. I could feed myself, wipe myself, and clothe myself. And I could walk. I guess you could say, I began to appreciate my life a little more.

My parents told me that no rent was due and to just work and save, save, save my money. My stepdad even made feminine-product shopping trips for me with no shame. Moments like this were when I believed that maybe not all men were as bad as I had seen or thought them to be.

I lived with my parents for the next few months before moving into my own small uninsulated downtown apartment. As I sat my parents down to tell them I was moving, I knew I had saved at least enough for two months' rent and deposit. There was no internet or cable, and I watched old movies on disk instead. I had no computer, just a Tracfone to mainly communicate with my parents. It was a cold and very small home, but it was mine. No other man was supporting me for once in my life.

I lived in my little apartment for about a year, and reflecting on my life, I really began to desire to know more of this God I had been hearing pieces of my entire life. Although the desire was there, my personal desires of life were more important at the time. I desired to have a husband, a family. In my little one-bedroom apartment, I still had no idea of this God too much, but I knew Satan pretty well.

Chapter 10

Satan's Fiery

One day in my apartment, I experienced the most demonic attack of my life. I was getting ready to shower when I felt a horrible stomach cramp. As I started to walk to my living room, I felt as if I was knocked down, which caused me to crawl to my recliner. Once there, I felt the recliner being pushed back. It lifted my feet off the floor, and a face appeared.

I was being held captive by Satan himself. I knew by the fiery red face, the overpowering strength over my body, and the heaviness on my chest. I was being choked with one fiery hand to the point that I couldn't scream for help, and with the other, I was being jabbed profusely in the stomach with something sharp. Suddenly, after what seemed like hours, it left. The chair flew forward, and the pressure on my throat lifted. This made my body feel weak and my mind feel distorted.

I was shaken. I could only think of calling my mom and explaining to her how much pain I was in. The only other person I thought to call was a boyfriend I broke up with a week prior. He came over to help me, as did my mom. I couldn't walk. I was shaking. My mom and my ex had to carry me down the stairs, and as they placed me in the backseat of Mom's car, I thought that with that kind of pain, something must be seriously wrong.

I was taken to the hospital, and after several tests, they found absolutely nothing wrong with me. I knew what happened to me, but Mom was right. If I mentioned it, they'd put me in a crazy-person ward.

I returned home and continued my life, hanging out with friends on weekends. My friends at that time were telling me about a social media site called MySpace. They mentioned that I could chat with old friends. So, wanting some kind of change in my single life, I drove to the local library down the street and began my new MySpace page containing butterflies and Mariah Carey music. A few times a week, I would go to the library and check my page. In the meantime, I worked my full-time job during the day and obtained a waitress job in the evenings.

One day, while at the library, a guy named Joe winked or whatever the code for "I'm interested" was. We began to chat online. At one point, he asked me for my phone number. Now let me inform you that I was *that* friend who never recommended meeting ANYONE online. And I told my friends not to meet them in person or they could kill you.

That was my belief anyways. My response to him asking me for my phone number was "How do I know that you're not some crazy psycho? What's your number?"

His response to me was "How do I know that *you're* not some crazy psycho?"

Fair enough. As I cleaned my small apartment, Joe and I spent time chatting about our jobs and family.

Finally, it was time to meet—in person! We met at Buffalo Wild Wings. As I pulled into the parking lot, I called him to see what type of car he was driving. He mentioned his car was a Mercedes. I mentioned mine was a green Sunfire. Butterflies filled my stomach.

At this moment, my grandma called to ask me to go to the grocery store for her, naming the many items on her list. I directed her to call Mom instead.

When I began to walk into the restaurant, I felt an overwhelming uncertainty. I saw a guy in a leather coat with a big beard, and he was quite a bit older than me. Suddenly, this wasn't looking like it was for me, like I wasn't feeling well, but Joe was actually standing behind him. Thank goodness!

As our eyes finally connected, we smiled at each other and ate dinner together. Bathroom trips for me that night were plenty as my friends who were in the bar as well would meet me there. They began speaking of how cute he was and to get his license plate number. This was familiar advice as it was something I had always told them to do for safety reasons.

Joe and I talked about our futures—futures of having our own families. I wanted a big family, much like mine. At this point in my life, I definitely knew what I did not want in a relationship. I asked him many questions: "What is your favorite color? How do you feel about your family? Have you been married before? Is there any chance you have any children out there?"

One conversation that sticks out was when he was staring at me. When I looked up and said "you're staring," his response was "I'm admiring." He mentioned having one sister and a stepbrother. His father had passed away in a car accident when he was two years old, and his mother had later married his stepdad. Joe never saw them as "stepfamily." He simply saw them as his dad and his brother.

The restaurant was closing soon, and as that night ended, we drove to see a movie—in his car, miles away. We began spending every day and night together. Whether it was at his house or mine, we enjoyed being together.

Joe entered the bathroom in my small apartment while I was doing my hair. As he got down on one knee, he asked if I would marry him. Problem was, it was a joke of his as he held out a blue snowflake ring he got from a cupcake at his grandparents' party.

It seemed too early for that question anyways!

With Joe, I felt a happiness and acceptance. He was caring and different from any man I had a relationship with previously.

It was at this time that I would be making some big life changes.

CHAPTER 11

Two Become One

Within that year, I relocated fourteen miles from my hometown to live in Joe's parents' small rental where he was living. It was a smaller apartment than mine with a big blue tote Joe used as a coffee table. It wasn't long before I had a pink hand towel in his bathroom, and I decorated his bachelor home with candles and flowers.

We loved playing board games and just being together. Bars, dancing, drinking, and the occasional weed smoking was our weekend fun. I smoked cigarettes from the age of eighteen while living with my best friend until Joe and I met. He didn't like the smell, and I didn't like the thought of my lungs being black, so I slowed down and then quit smoking.

A funny smoking story I shared with him was that when I was living with my best friend, one day, we desired a cigarette so badly. With lack of change or cash, we went to the Harley-Davidson "wall of fame" that her stepdad displayed on their living room wall. There was a pack of cigarettes, unopened. We put a little hole in the package and slid out one cigarette. That was the stalest cig we ever smoked, and later, I would be condemned enough to confess this horrible act to her stepdad—at church.

Joe and I had a roller-coaster relationship. We loved but didn't fully appreciate each other. At times, we called each other names, resulting in arguments. These disagreements were usually settled quickly with forgiveness. We lived in the apartment but soon moved into a duplex Joe had purchased before we met. He worked as a personal trainer for a gym in Columbus before working as a construction worker for his dad. I left my job in my hometown and began to work as an aide at the elementary school. It was a job I loved since I enjoyed kids so much.

Although we had a slightly toxic relationship of not fully respecting each other, the good greatly overshadowed the bad, so we decided to tie the knot. Joe asked me to marry him during one of our game nights, on my birthday. He entered the room, got down on one knee, and began to tell me how much he loved me. He then pulled a box from his pocket and handed it to me with shaking hands. I opened the box, saw the ring, and in my excitement, I threw the ring. After searching the room, we found the ring under the bed. No joke this time! I was finally going to get married!

Shortly after becoming engaged, Joe and I moved into a duplex he had acquired before we met. It was our first remodeling job together. From sanding hardwood floors to painting walls, the duplex soon began to feel like a home. I had multiple shopping trips and finally found my wedding dress with the help of our mothers and sisters. It was a beautiful mermaid-style lace dress with a very long train. I sent out the invites and began to plan for our big day!

The day of the wedding, I had butterflies in my belly. Although we had our negative moments, I was so happy to be marrying Joe. He called it a highlighter wedding. Our colors were neon blue, pink, green, and yellow, with daisies being the dominant flower. With the decorations in place, some hearts were displaced. It was hard for Joe's mom to allow another woman she didn't fully know to marry her son. On our wedding day, I had to give her my word that I loved her son and that he wasn't making a mistake. It was like anything and everything was against us getting married. After a friend called and said she couldn't be at the wedding and her daughter wouldn't be our flower girl due to car issues she was experiencing, we quickly had to find others. Why was this wedding not looking so good?

I called my stepmom, whom I communicated with concerning my siblings, and my baby sisters stayed the night before the wedding. We had bought their dresses at Peebles and Walmart the day before. Joe's best man was his brother, and my maid of honor was my sister. The groomsmen were Joe's friends, and my bridesmaids were my sisters and Joe's sister. Our flower girl was my baby sister who was wearing a cast from a previous injury, and there was no ring bearer as my nephew was too young. It was all finally coming together!

I was ushered down the aisle by my grandma, who was my best friend. She kept stepping on my dress, smiling at me as we walked arm in arm. Guests were ushered up in golf carts as Joe's family loved their golf.

Our wedding was held on the eighteenth hole of the golf course. The moment the ceremony began, I had tunnel vision and could only see Joe at that moment. His eyes filled up with tears, as did mine. On a beautiful sunshiny day (June 19, 2010), we were married by Joe's cousin. We were surrounded by our friends and family as we began our life together.

Joe and I enjoyed a beautiful reception at the clubhouse of the golf course, followed by a late reception at Baker's Pizza. We attended this party in our wedding attire and were served more alcohol shots than we could ever drink. The wedding night, we stayed at a local hotel as I knew if I went home, I would just begin chores. Laundry would not be happening on our wedding day.

The day following the wedding, feeling a little hungover and tired, we didn't leave for our honeymoon as originally planned. Our home looked like Christmas from all the wedding gifts.

Knowing we were driving to Florida to visit Disney World, we finally began the drive. Disney was so much fun! Since I was the oldest of so many kids, it had always been a desire of mine, and Joe was making it happen! The characters at Disney noticed my shirt, which read "just hitched," and they began joking with us being newlyweds. While admiring Magic Kingdom, we joined the crowd as the parade passed. We even saw the night fireworks over the castle. Everything was timed just right, and it was so magical!

In our hotel, we had so many ham sandwiches as we had accumulated many Walmart gift cards as wedding gifts. It saved us money on food so we could enjoy more exciting activities.

Finally, we were now sharing the same last name—that tough, long last name I had to learn how to spell. Writing my new last name on wedding checks was pretty weird, but in a good way.

CHAPTER 12

The Call

Joe and I enjoyed our lives as one, spending time with family and friends. Oftentimes on the weekends, we would have my niece and nephew stay with us overnight. Being an aunt and uncle brought us so much happiness. Three of my father's kids would stay for weekends too, especially at Christmas, my favorite holiday. We made gingerbread houses and decorated cookies with my siblings.

Other activities included bedtime stories, Play-Doh, water slides, and tickle monsters. It seemed as if every weekend, we had kids over to visit and play.

Occasionally, Grandma would come and stay in our little guest room with bunk beds. Joe always cooked a great huge breakfast. Grandma loved the bacon the most and enjoyed being treated as a queen by Joe and me. We were sure to make her feel special as it was obvious from her health getting worse that we could lose her any day. This was a hard reality for me. At the young age of forty-three, we got the call that my uncle had pneumonia again—only this time, his body wouldn't recover. We were pretty close as I was my mom's eldest child.

My heart broke as I stood over him in his casket, and I began to ask myself so many questions. Why did he die so young? What were my grandma and mom going to do after losing a son and a brother?

His funeral was the first funeral I had been to, and the pain I felt was so undeniable. Especially when my uncle who was born mentally challenged went up to his casket and asked him, "Why did you have to leave me?" His passing was very hard on Grandma too. She cried often, saying she missed him so much.

Grandma and I loved his laugh and contagious happiness for life despite his physical condition. I think upon the good memories and know how faithful he was, having no doubt that my uncle is now with our Savior, complete and healed.

My grandma was my best friend until I met Joe. During these times that Grandma stayed, she and I would reminisce about my childhood memories at her and Grandpa's house. Those childhood moments gave me so much respect for her and Grandpa.

I spent as much time as I could with my grandma. Joe and I drove her to visit my other uncle, who enjoyed the visits as well. The road trips were becoming harder for Grandma as her health began to decline. She went from sitting up front to lying in the back seat many times due to not feeling well.

In the upcoming months, we would find out that my grandma had stage 4 lung cancer. It seemed likely since she told us of smoking her first cigarette at the age of eight, although it was still a very hard truth for my siblings and me to accept. Doctors gave her a few months to live; however, we enjoyed another four years with her, appreciating every moment.

My siblings and I took turns visiting Grandma in her little apartment or, as she called it, her "castle on the hill." My mom took care of the grocery shopping for Grandma as we all seemed to appreciate her more. Grandma took full advantage of this and would make us feel guilty, stating that no one visited her although one of us had just left her home.

She made sure to send us to a gas station to get her lottery tickets or a trip to the pizza shop. We were all just happy that Grandma finally quit smoking. I believe she quit so quickly at the fear of a lung cancer diagnosis.

One day while at work, I got the call that Grandma had a stroke. Mom, through tears, told me that Grandma's caregiver went to check on her, and she was lying helpless on her bedroom floor. Scared as to what might happen next, I rushed over to the emergency room, and there I saw Grandma lying in a hospital bed. She could speak but was very weak in her voice and movements. I held her hand and asked her, "Grandma, are you okay?"

She quietly replied, "Yes, honey, I'm okay."

It was clear to me that no matter what she was saying, Grandma was not okay. It was obvious to me that she was in a lot of pain.

I thought it would be a good idea at this time to call my brother's family. My niece and nephew told Grandma they loved her. Grandma softly spoke that she loved them too. I wasn't sure what was happening to Grandma or if she would even get better to return home at this point.

My siblings, Mom, and I were talking about Grandma possibly going into a nursing home once she left the emergency room. We began to schedule when we would visit and check in on her daily. All at once, I observed my grandma open her eyes so big, and she smiled. She looked so beautiful like the photo on her living room wall—a younger her. She then clearly spoke two words. She said, "Hi, God." Then she closed her eyes peacefully like she just saw God himself standing before her. It was the most amazing sight to witness.

Chapter 13

Amazing Grace

Grandma's health wasn't improving, so Mom decided it was best to have her transported. She would be taken to a hospital for better care and observation. Mom was Grandma's power of attorney, so she became Grandma's decision-maker. I felt it was a good choice. Grandma could receive more thorough care for her stroke. She was driven to the hospital a few miles away. Joe and I drove ourselves to the hospital.

Once we arrived, we heard the hospital staff mention what floor Grandma would be on. It was called the "end-of-life unit." At first, I thought I misheard them and thought she just had a stroke. How could she be dying now? The doctor began to prepare her for surgery to remove a clot. During this time, Grandma began to have mini heart attacks, resulting in no surgery. She was being placed in a room to keep her at peace. Her health had dramatically declined, and she no longer had her eyes open much, rather closed and in a sleeplike state. I began to cry, begging the God I had heard about. "God, please don't take my grandma, my best friend. She means the world to me."

In the hospital room, my siblings and I began to talk among each other about when we were kids playing in Grandma and Grandpa's backyard. We talked about everything, not noticing that our grandma—our second mom, in a sense—lay brain dead in the bed next to us. The nurses told us that she could still hear us until her last breath was breathed, that it was good to talk about the good memories. She could hear us.

The hospital staff was so accommodating to Grandma and our family. My parents, my four siblings, Joe, and I spent the night in the hospital with Grandma that night. I lay by her side, curled up in a hard wooden chair. I was squeezing her hand, and my brother lay in the bed near her head with his hand resting on her heart. Throughout that night, we didn't get much sleep at all as she would stop breathing. My brother and I sat up and looked at each other with tear-filled eyes as we would count up to forty seconds until she would begin to breathe again. Her heart would stop, and we would cry, asking her to stay with us. It was the toughest, most heartbreaking night ever.

The next morning, she was still breathing off and on, and her heart was pumping then suddenly stopping and starting.

Joe and my siblings were going to go home to shower and grab some more clothes. We did not know how long we would be in this room while Grandma lay unresponsive. Joe kept asking if I was sure about him leaving. I said, "Yes, my parents are here. I will be fine." He left, as did all my siblings, saying they would return later after showers and packing more clothes.

Grandma became weaker as her breathing stopped much longer, and her heart stopped more often. The nurses asked if we wanted a piece of her hair or fingerprint. We didn't need any of that with the wonderful memories we had. Besides, about two years prior, I sat down with Grandma and recorded her as I asked her questions about her life. And at the end, she left a message to her kids and grandkids. It was something I knew we needed to do. It would be hard to do at that moment, but it would be great for our kids and her future grandkids.

I began to pray, asking God once more to help her live. God spoke to me at this very moment, and in a soft but stern voice, he told me to stop being selfish. To let her go to heaven and to let her know it's going to be okay.

As Grandma lay there weak and with her eyes closed, I began to speak differently to her. I said to her, "Grandma, you can go. We will miss you, but you have struggled long enough. Let go, Grandma. It's okay."

I cried my eyes out speaking these words to her. I was saying the words as my heart was shattering inside my chest. This woman was there for me when I was a child, and she was the one woman I had felt safe with my entire life. And now I had to watch her leave me forever.

My stepdad, heartbroken by the situation, went into the hall to pray. To ask God to just end this misery for her. She adored him and was happy my mom had chosen him as her husband, and he also did a lot for Grandma.

Mom and I were in the room, holding each other and holding Grandma's hand. Staring at the woman we both loved so much, we knew we would soon only have each other.

Grandma made a gasping noise, and I knew this was it. She was letting go and going to meet her maker. I let out the loudest cry and stormed to the window in her room.

I watched outside as the snow fell harder than it had prior to this day. This cold January day, I would be saying goodbye to the woman I was so close to. The woman who never judged me or put me down, who loved me unconditionally. I knew this was the end of our conversations in her little apartment as we would sit in her recliner together and just talk. This was it. Grandma's life was coming to an end. As I watched her life fade, all I could think about was the good memories I had with her. She helped me to feel accepted and very loved. Because of this it hurt more to have to tell her goodbye.

Mom then said, "Brandy, come here. Grandma's last tear is falling."

The nurses had let us know that at times, the last tear can be seen, but not often.

I walked over to Grandma and held her lifeless hand as I witnessed her last tear fall from her eyes onto her pillow. Mom and

I cried and held each other. This was something I knew Grandma would have been glad to see.

My stepdad came into the room, and Joe came in a short time later. I heard a minister enter the room while I was crying in a corner. He laid his hand on my shoulder and began to pray. I was heartbroken.

How could I actually let go? Joe asked if I wanted to leave the room for a minute, so we walked down the hall to a big lobby. I sat in a chair with him and cried many tears as he held me. I noticed a piano in the corner, and as I lay there crying, I saw a nurse wearing all white—white hat, coat, stockings, and shoes. She walked over to the piano, and the room was suddenly filled with Grandma's favorite song, "Amazing Grace." I thought that it was so nice that the staff did that when a patient passed.

The only concerning part was that although I saw and heard this, *no one else did*.

That day in the hospital was the first day I believe I really felt the presence of God. Although we had just said goodbye to Grandma, my best friend, there was an overwhelming peace within us all.

CHAPTER 14

Endo

The funeral was very rough for my mother as now, she had lost a father, a brother, and now a mother. Decisions had to be made concerning Grandma's belongings.

Shortly after the funeral, my mother, my siblings, and I walked into Grandma's apartment to discuss and disperse Grandma's belongings. There was no disagreement about what would happen to her possessions as we saw in other family deaths. We just knew if it was something that none of us really needed, my brother would gladly take it. He took every little item, every piece of Grandma he could get, as losing her weighed heavily on him. This made him feel closer to her, and for every item we didn't want, he yelled, "I'll take it!"

We were all united as a family through this difficult time. We realized that my grandma was the backbone that held our family together as Mom and I had many conversations about her. Once, my mom mentioned that while staying at Grandma's home one night, she heard her praying. She was praying in her bed for her family—praying out loud until she would begin snoring as she fell asleep. Hearing about my grandma praying for me made me thankful as

I thought that she could have been the help, rescuing me so many times throughout my life. I wanted to know this God that Grandma had prayed to, whom I had recently heard speaking to me during her death. I knew my grandma was in heaven with God.

Not only did I want to know this God, my desire to be a mother grew even stronger. I desperately wanted to know what it was like to feel a baby growing in my belly, but it wasn't happening. I had multiple doctor appointments for stomach pain, and no diagnosis was found to be the source of my pain. Finding no reason for the terrible cramps, I couldn't help but think that my discomfort was a result of past circumstances. Was it possible that due to the very strict bathroom schedule as a teenager, I was having trouble? Or could it have been because of the demotic attack in my apartment when I felt that Satan himself was stabbing me? Could I have pain due to secretly being given birth control from the age of fifteen to eighteen?

Although I had many questions, I decided to visit a professional to assess my issues. During one doctor appointment, they found a large cyst on my ovaries and were concerned about the size. They recommended a surgery, which revealed that I had endometriosis. This was described as a disorder where the tissue that makes up the uterine lining of the womb grows outside the uterus. It is usually found in the lower abdomen or pelvis and has symptoms of horrible pain. This torment was one I had for the majority of my life, not knowing it was an abnormal suffering. I thought that every woman's monthly cycle of discomfort was like mine. I would lie on the floor and grab my belly in tears, and sometimes I'd be screaming. The pain came at the most inconvenient times. In the grocery store, during photo shoots, or in our home, the pain was always showing up. I couldn't prepare for it. I just had to learn to live with it.

Joe felt bad that no matter what he did, my pain would continue even after the surgery. Heat and pressure helped, as did painkillers. I had to be very careful as pills were something I was addicted to prior to meeting Joe. Endometriosis would be a hindrance in my life; however, there was a strong desire to become a mother and make our living quarters a home. We wanted this for our hopeful child, and it became our focus. We were ready to prioritize life and strengthen our careers.

At this time, we noticed a small lump on my right breast, and surgery was necessary. Luckily though, the lump was a benign cyst that the doctor carefully removed. I was thankful this was nothing serious and in time would heal, leaving a small scar on my breast.

In 2014, we were living in Joe's duplex that we remodeled together. We had slowed down on our partying and focused more on our jobs and home. Joe had begun his own business with a business partner where they remodeled or built upon new properties. One of my jobs at this time was assisting Joe's grandparents with household chores every morning since his grandma had a stroke shortly following our wedding. I helped her with exercising and cleaned their home. I also began my photography business as my passion for taking photos as a child began with Grandma's 110 camera. I set up props such as laundry detergent and mops. I then posed my young siblings next to the cleaning supplies, assisting them in looking tired from a day of hard work. Rosebushes became beautiful backgrounds as I added roses to their hair.

This photo passion became a reality as I proceeded to open a studio in a small garage, progressing to a warehouse owned by Joe's dad. Later, I actually owned my own downtown photography studio.

The day Joe took me to the bank to get the key, I could hardly believe that I had gone from doing photo shoots in our dining room to owning my own downtown studio! He used the back of the building as storage for tools to operate with his business partner. Not long after we acquired the downtown building, we began to remodel the upstairs as well. With the help of our friends and family, our new home came to life.

It was an old modern loft home with large windows overlooking downtown. The photo studio and loft home included five bathrooms. There was a master bed and bath along with two other bedrooms with a jack-and-jill bathroom connecting them. One room would prayerfully be a nursery one day. The other room was my craft room. It was our home sweet home.

I slowly began to acquire clientele for my business. I wanted to have affordable photos for families as I saw how much it cost to get my senior photos when I graduated. I couldn't afford them, so my senior photos consisted of about five photos from the Walmart photo department. We were so busy getting this part of our life together that the desire of becoming parents was overshadowed. I felt like the more I stayed busy doing things, the easier it was to pretend I was okay not being a mother. We were trying to get our lives together for the betterment of our future family.

CHAPTER 15

Accepted Sinner

Joe and I were living life the best way we knew how. Still wanting to be parents, we had no success after approximately four years. I was beginning to wonder if I would ever be a mom. It was a childhood dream of mine, and I always wanted a house full of kids. Joe wanted to be a dad.

In 2014, Joe began to read his Bible. It was something I had never seen him do before.

Suddenly, he didn't want to have a drink with me. He didn't want to go to the bar at all. He didn't want to be a part of gossip or slander anymore. He was becoming someone I didn't know. The change in Joe was so contrasting, I had begun to question if we should be married any longer. I mean, we were different people, and I was quite happy living the life I was living.

The word *divorce* began to be on my lips more often. I couldn't understand why he was suddenly treating me so well. He had been okay to me prior, but this was different. He began respecting me and was concerned about how I felt. This was so unfamiliar to me. I began to question him and ask him why he changed. I asked him why he was suddenly so nice to me. Up until now, most of the men I knew treated me poorly and made me feel unimportant. He told me that he finally listened to THE voice.

I asked, "What voice?"

He said, "The voice of God."

This was intriguing. There was that God again. He also described him as love, as did my stepdad.

Joe told me that he was saved and was recommitting his life to Christ. I knew of this from when I was prayed over as a preteen at the church we went to occasionally. I told him that night in our bed that I didn't know if I was saved or not. I thought that if I actually desired to be saved, I needed to find a church and have the people there pray over me.

He then told me that I could be saved right then and there in the comfort of our bedroom. Joe prayed with me and read me the sinner's prayer from the Bible as I repeated after him. That night, I asked Jesus into my heart. I asked him to forgive me of my sins.

I can't really put into words the weight I immediately felt lifted off my shoulders. It was a heaviness on my shoulders that I felt disappear.

This one choice, this one night, would change my life forever.

From the moment of recommitting his life to Christ, Joe began to look into churches to attend. When he asked me to consider attending one as his wife, my comment to him was "I don't need to go to church to be a Christian, and I'm not ever going to go to one of them big churches on Route 4."

He explained to me that one pastor had preached a sermon from a tree stand. Joe knew, since I loved watching *Duck Dynasty* on TV, this would interest me.

One day, as I sat in the office of my studio viewing the sermon on my computer, it was like the pastor was talking directly to me. I then told Joe I would be interested in going to church with him. One time.

So the following Sunday, we set off to church. I was dressed like an older lady as I showed up with my knees and elbows covered. This was what I remembered from the church I went to when I was a child. I soon realized that this church had all types of people. Some wore jeans, and others dressed in suits. There was no dress code. I was an accepted sinner.

During the praise-and-worship part of this visit, I became very ill and had to leave the church service. Because of this experience, I felt like knowing additional information about God.

I asked Joe if we could visit this church the following Sunday. His response was "They have Wednesday services too."

And so it began. As we attended more services, we met other Christians who lived the Christian life. Eventually, we became a part of weekly Bible studies and other church activities. This was what I had been missing: people who loved God in the same room, worshiping him and praising him. I felt like this was just where Jesus wanted me to be.

Joe and I began friendships with other Christians, wanting a deeper relationship with God. As these relationships progressed, I began attending women's events such as Joyce Meyers and Chonda Pierce. My studio quickly became the setting for a women's Bible study and a once-a-month connect for life group.

A short time after we began attending the church, Joe's parents did also. His mom and I began a healthy loving relationship.

Joe became an usher at church, and I began to help in the children's ministry. We became members, attending every Sunday and Wednesday, and we began to change how we treated each other. We appreciated each other much more than we had in the past. The drinking that had continued on occasion and all the smoking ended.

I began to organize our house as if it was cleaning our minds. Negative movies and songs came to an end, and we began to make God the center of our lives.

I was ready to put my old life behind me and try to live my life in a way that God would be proud of. I felt strong in my spirit as I organized my priorities in life.

CHAPTER 16

Expected Guest

Throughout these major life changes that we were undergoing, Joe and I stayed in contact with my dad's three kids, who were now teenagers. They had a rough life as our dad was in prison for most of their childhood as well. This reminded me of my experience as his daughter. When he wasn't in prison, he was fighting with their mom and drinking.

During one conversation with his youngest daughter (my flower girl at our wedding), my sister told me that both her parents were going to jail and that she would have to go to foster care. This sister who mentioned foster care I remember caring for as a baby. My stepmom was pregnant with her when I was eighteen. She spent a lot of time with me, and some people thought she was *my* child. She did somewhat look like me, having the same dad and all.

Joe and I had also communicated about possibly having to help one of my siblings at some point in their lives. He witnessed their life too, so he agreed to that possibility. When my baby sister had mentioned foster care, we set up a lunch date.

My aunt, my sister, and I met for lunch at a local restaurant close to where she lived. At that time, she was living with her aunt and uncle (my dad's brother). I explained to my sister that if anyone mentioned foster care again, to let them know she had an older sister and brother-in-law whom she could live with.

It wasn't long after that conversation that she came to live with us. She was beyond excited to live with Joe and her big sister! She said she had always wanted to live with us. Some of the fun things we did included taking snow photo shoots, crafting, listening to music, and going to church. She began going to church about the same time Joe and I did—on Wednesday evenings as well as Sunday mornings. Joe helped her with her homework, especially her confusing math lessons.

We wanted my baby sister to feel loved and cared for, and we prayed with her, consoling her when she longed for her mom and dad. We had the same dad, so I could sympathize with her more. My sister's mom did not show up to most of her appointed visits. This would result in my little sister sitting in her bed and crying on multiple occasions. I enjoyed hugging and praying with her as I could understand the pain of her parents not being in her life. I had the same pain as a teenager, so I could relate to her in our conversations.

Our family also accepted her in their lives as they knew she was now a big part of ours. Joe's mom and dad helped plan a fun shopping trip for her as she didn't have much when she came to stay with us. Her clothes had holes, and her shoes were too small and also had holes. We supplied her with all she needed and many things that she wanted as well. Most of all, we tried showing her God's love as we were learning it. This was when we no longer entertained drinking, cursing, negative movies, or music, leaving her with a positive environment. Despite the unpleasant phone calls we received from my sister's parents and other family members, or the court visits or the threats, our goal was to give her a positive experience for as long as God had intended.

Moving in a few weeks prior, I signed my sister up for church teen functions. She reluctantly traveled to church camp and had a gratifying weekend. It was more fun than she first thought was possible. This made us excited for her and her future as she began to acquire friendships with other teenage girls at church.

Joe and I had to mature rapidly during this process of having a teenager in our home. We made sure that we did not speak negatively about her parents in front of her. We were personally disgusted by some of their acts; however, we never expressed them to her as she was dealing with enough issues of her own. She felt like her parents could care for her even with their addictions to drugs and alcohol.

As the negative conversations between my sister and her mom continued, she continued to push further away from Joe and me. She missed her parents and wanted to live with them even though they were not stable enough to parent her.

Setting my own feelings and thoughts of my father aside, we took my sister to visit him in rehab. I hadn't even seen my dad in years, but I knew she loved him and that I would have to do this to help her see that we truly cared for her.

About six months after living with us, just before her fourteenth birthday, my sister told us she didn't want to live with us anymore. We believed that our rules and consistency were too unfamiliar to her. At her new school, she was beginning healthy friendships, and her grades improved from Ds and Fs to merit roll (all As and Bs.)

I was a little shocked to hear she wanted to leave our home, but I knew it was a high possibility in her confused young mind.

Taking her to church to hear God's word and loving her was all we could do. And we prayed that somehow, she would take some of the good she required with her when she did leave. She moved out that night to quickly journey back to her parents' home.

Approximately one year from when my sister moved out, her parents called us to apologize for their adverse behavior. It deeply saddened me to see a child being tossed into the system the way we saw it firsthand.

The day she left, I was heartbroken. I thought we could help her more than what we did. I had failed.

Chapter 17

Fertility Baggage

Following my sister moving out of our home, Joe and I continued going to church and spending time with family. We were still unable to conceive and begin a family, so part of me felt like I was being teased by God. I was given a child in my home for a short six months to care for. But that mothering bone deep within had grown even more. I wanted to be a mother so badly. This caused frustrations in our marriage because I felt inadequate as a wife and as a woman. Everywhere I looked, I saw pregnant women. It wasn't something I could escape. My prayers went up, but still, I thought God was not noticing me. Like the woman in the Bible story who just got a touch of the hem of his garment as he passed, I felt like he had passed me up. I was just here, waiting.

As the low self-esteem rose in me, our marriage began to stumble once more. I felt as if Joe deserved a woman who could give him a baby. When we were around kids, they embraced Joe. He loved them, and I could tell that he would be the best daddy ever. He was already the best husband I could have ever asked for. My husband loves God so much, and he reads and prays daily. His faith is never lacking.

Joe was adamant that God had a very special child for us. That this child would do amazing things for the kingdom.

Although I wanted to believe him, I still had my doubts. Not only was I feeling unworthy as a woman, friends and family began to tiptoe around the baby and pregnancy conversations because they knew these would hurt me.

One day at Joe's parents' house, his brother and wife visited as we all did on Sundays. This was a different visit. They handed each of his parents a box with a cake inside. This was to announce that they were expecting! Emotion overload. I was happy for them and overjoyed for Joe's parents to finally become grandparents, but I was also confused and feeling so broken in some sort of bondage. I know it bothered my sister-in-law to tell us about the pregnancy, but I'm very thankful they did. It helped me with the feeling of being "left out."

On departing from my in-laws' home, I wailed out and even began to yell at God. I began questioning God as to why he was doing this to me. At times, I would even describe myself to Joe that I was *broken*.

Shortly after, one Sunday morning, I went to church, and I felt a strong pull to go to the altar. It was so powerful. I stayed with my feet planted firmly on the floor, but I couldn't fight this tug any longer. As I walked up to the altar, my surroundings were clear and white. It was like it was just God and me at that altar. Nothing or no none else mattered in that moment. As tears constantly dropped from my eyes, I handed this fertility burden to God. I could no longer carry the depression of not bearing a child anymore. I was giving it to God. It was like I handed it right to him, and he welcomed it with open arms.

After I had thrown off the pregnancy baggage, I began to notice changes in myself. Baby showers were once again happening, and life became fun again. No more shame or doubt cluttered my mind. I began to believe that God would answer our prayers when his timing was right—not mine.

I began designing a small "faith box" that was a cardboard box consisting of baby lotions, soaps, wipes, diapers, and one special onesie I had created that read "I'm here because of Jesus and prayers." I purchased items only when I felt that God was telling me to purchase them. I prayed over every item added to the faith box and decided to live by faith and not by sight. I might not have been able to see God, but I definitely heard and felt him ever so close to me.

Continuing doctor visits to help with the random discomfort I was experiencing very often, the sharp stabs continued. The sharpness went from hurting just around the time of my menstrual cycle to feeling it come out of nowhere while carrying out daily activities. It was a pain that would stop me in my tracks.

The doctor decided to do another surgery to remove any endometriosis—this time, in a well-known hospital specializing in it rather than a general hospital. I went into this surgery with much prayer. I couldn't attend the Joyce Meyer conference as that was on the day of my surgery; however, I felt the prayers of the ladies from our church who did go.

Joe was by my side the entire time, praying over me constantly. After hours of surgery, doctors found that I had stage 4 endometriosis and prescribed me birth control for a few months to regulate my cycle and alleviate the pain.

In my weeks of recovery, Joe cared for me so lovingly. He helped me shower and cooked for me. Some of the items he helped me shower with came from my baby faith box as I could only use light soaps on the lacerations on my belly. We even tried a few rounds of IUI, where they would insert my husband's sperm directly into my uterus. Three cycles with no luck of pregnancy.

Doctors still couldn't give an explanation as to why we were not getting pregnant but gave us information to begin the in vitro process. This consisted of combining an egg and sperm in a laboratory dish then transplanting it to the woman's uterus, and this was the one chance where we could actually become pregnant! I felt hopeful and excited that maybe this is how I become a mommy finally.

As we began navigating through the in vitro process, I continued meeting with women and testifying to, hopefully, encourage someone else who may be going through a similar experience. I was no longer experiencing the stabbing in my lower stomach as I did before the surgery. Yes, there were still other struggles in my life, but now my hurdles of life were overcome with the help of God himself.

We began to be prayed over at church, and a few times, we were prophesied that we would conceive a child of my womb…and a child not of my womb, whatever that meant.

Our marriage began to thrive as we met with other Christian couples who loved God. Our communication grew stronger.

Joe began going to men's conferences, and one weekend, when he was at one event, I began to look further into adoption. The ads were constantly popping up on my Facebook. Out of curiosity, I called a few of the agencies and requested more information. I began to talk to God about this inquiry. When Joe returned from his weekend conference, we sat down, and through many tears, I told him that I had prayed and was feeling strongly against the in vitro process. It was our one chance to be parents, and I was feeling so strongly against it!

This was one of the heaviest feelings I had ever felt. It was like God, my heavenly father, was telling me, "No! Absolutely not."

I didn't understand why God was telling me I couldn't do the one thing that could make me become a mother. I was hurt and, once again, felt broken. Every day, I walked past mothers—mothers who loved their children and mothers who neglected their children. Oftentimes, I thought about the love I had in my heart to give to a child if only given the chance.

Chapter 18

For This Child I Prayed

Joe held me as I cried, knowing that God really didn't want me to do IVF. During a prayer, I heard God in a still small voice telling me that I should not to do this procedure. I had such a healthy fear of God that I knew if I had done what he was against, it wouldn't end well. It had to be his plan, not mine. Then quietly, he asked, "Have you ever thought about adoption?" He was careful in asking this, knowing it was something that we had not discussed prior to now.

To me, this would mean that, sadly, we were accepting that we wouldn't ever be conceiving a child. I did have a desire, an interest, in adoption ever since I was a child playing with baby dolls. There was always something special about it to me. I admired how people could love a child not of their body or blood.

This intrigued us. At that moment, it felt like we were standing in the middle of a circle with ten thousand paths stretching from it. Where do we go from here?

Joe and I began to communicate all our options to each other. We conversed with other people to help us decide what steps to take next concerning adoption.

Things began to look hopeful for our futures, and sometimes this was sparked by interactions with other people. While working in my studio one day, a woman came in asking if I would sponsor a young family member of hers who had recently passed. She was placing bracelets in storefronts to raise money for awareness.

The following week, I agreed to meet with her in a local coffee shop at her request. Just a few days before meeting with her, I had a dream.

In this dream, my grandma and my grandpa, along with my uncle David, were passing a baby back and forth in heaven. The view was so white and beautiful. My grandma, smiling, passed the baby to my grandpa, and my grandpa then passed the baby to Jesus. I saw Jesus's legs, feet, and hands only. He cradled his hands as the baby was placed in them. Jesus then turned to a cloud and placed the baby carefully into the cloud.

Suddenly, I awoke crying. I was startled and amazed. I saw my baby. I saw my family. I saw part of Jesus! It was the craziest dream I had ever had. I called my mom and Joe about the dream. They were amazed as well.

When the lady called to schedule our exact meeting, we began to have some conversations about babies. She was told she couldn't have kids, and although I personally never heard those specific words, we had similar stories. She had a strong faith and bought things like baby carriers and such.

The meeting was set, and we met at the local coffee shop. She carried a gift bag in with her along with the bracelets to sell in my studio. We had a great conversation, and as it came to an end, the baby talk came up once more. For some reason, I then felt the need to tell her about my dream. About seeing a baby cradled in Jesus's hands, sat into a cloud.

She began to cry. Through her tears, she handed me the bag and said, "I have kept this item on my nightstand for years, and I believe

God has wanted me to give it to you since we talked. You won't believe what is in the bag."

I opened the bag, only to find a ceramic baby cradled by hands, just like in my dream! On the front, it read, "For this child I prayed."

I cried as she asked me, "Is this what you saw in your dream?"

It was so amazing, and we sat there crying and holding each other. God was putting people directly in my path.

Joe was so shocked by this when I arrived home and told him what had happened. We both knew we had to pray about what to do next.

As we prayed to God and held on to the adoption path, we decided to gather more information about our options. Joe mentioned his friend at church who had a sister that worked for a faith-based adoption agency in Ohio. We called the agency, and after letting them know we were interested in knowing more, they prayed with us over the phone, two potential souls with the desire to be parents.

Shortly after, we scheduled our first adoption class with other parents who were also interested in adopting. Our car at that time had to go in for some work, so we borrowed his friend's van so that we could attend our session. Joe's friend owned a car lot, so he had one we could use for our trip.

As we headed out for our very first adoption class, WHAM! A deer came toward us on the highway and somehow smacked into the driver's side, leaving a huge dent in it and causing the outside mirror to come loose. It hung out of the window as we drove to our class.

Great start to this process, we thought. This was just one of the enemy's tactics to keep us from adopting one of God's children.

As I sat in the class looking down at my purse, I saw a ball of deer hair on it! Gross! The people in our class laughed with us and prayed for safe travels home.

We were given packets of information to take home concerning the adoption process.

CHAPTER 19

God's Grace

In the next few months, we had to fill out a ton of paperwork, including forms of what you would or would not consider when adopting a child. The birth mom could have had an alcohol problem or a heroin problem or some other drug addiction. If you checked that box, you wouldn't even consider her child even if she used it one time, and then this could slow down the process dramatically. We also had to consider the sex and ethnicity of our child.

Through much prayer together, we chose to not have preference on the sex or ethnicity of our baby. We simply prayed for a healthy baby. Joe and I had conversations with family members about our decision, and although some didn't fully agree with all our decisions, they accepted our choice.

We had to have a home study completed by the adoption agency. During this process, they accessed our home to make sure the house was adequate for a child to occupy. We also received background checks and classes with many life questions. One class was about adopting a child of another race. We had to consider all potential issues or situations.

I had always had a deep, deep desire to have a baby girl, but what was coming out of my mouth to people was the opposite. I was ready to accept whatever God had for us!

We were finally at the point in the process to create a scrapbook for our birth mom. This would help her better decide on who she wanted to parent her child. It was to include photos of our friends and family and what we did for fun. Up until this point, we had many photos containing all races and genders to add to our book. I worked on creating a perfect book as I loved to craft.

Joe took care of the adoption paperwork—every piece that came our way. I knew he was ready to be a daddy as much as I was ready to be a mommy. We were told it could be weeks, months, or even years before we would get a call to adopt.

Now in the process of adoption, we waited until, one day, Joe called me with the best news ever! When he called, I was at my sister's house with my mom and my oldest sister. I was helping them host my baby sister's bridal shower.

My baby sister was visiting from her home in Florida. She had a beautiful bridal shower, and the night ended with all us sisters and Mom cuddling on the couch as we did many times.

It was time for me to drive home. As I began to pull out of her driveway, I received a call from Joe, who said, "Honey, they have a birth mom who wants to meet us!"

I could not believe what he was saying as I parked the car and ran back into my sister's house crying tears of joy and experiencing some disbelief! I was feeling a little anxious as our book wasn't even done yet for the birth mom! We were going to be meeting her in two days! But only if we agreed to accept a baby girl of another race.

Not one thing felt wrong with this! I cried the entire drive home, praising God along the way. He was showing us his grace and goodness.

Then some fears began to set in. What if the birth mom didn't like us? Were we prepared to meet our birth mom?

When I arrived home, Joe and I prayed together and asked God to give us discernment and to just allow us to be ourselves. Two days later, we drove to meet her! Joe and I ate lunch at Wendy's, and as we sat in the car waiting to meet our potential birth mom for the first time, I felt a nervousness come over me. It was a very real "I'm going to throw up" feeling. I called a friend for prayer. Just talking to someone in my circle helped to calm me.

Walking into the agency, I asked Joe if we were allowed to hug her. How were we to react? I was going crazy, but I also had so much excitement!

As we entered the room, I saw two ladies from the agency and a beautiful young woman, tall and smaller in stature. I walked up to her and put both my hands on her cheeks. The words that came out of my mouth were "Oh my gosh! You are so beautiful."

I hugged her, feeling her large baby bump press against my belly. Joe hugged her, and we sat on a couch across from her.

The room had a wall of crosses, and I felt God's peace in that moment. We were introduced by the agency staff, and all she and I could do was look at each other and smile so much. It was an instant connection that I can't really explain.

Like a sister or family connection but different somehow. I held on tightly to the scrapbook that we constructed just two days prior! The scrapbook had pink sparkles on it, and as I sat there showing it to her, the color from the book began to bleed onto our hands because we were sweating from our nerves. She told Joe and me that she was okay with it because pink was her favorite color too!

We had so many similarities. Our lives were slightly different from each other, and we both had disappointments, but I knew God had brought us together on this day for this exact moment. We had heard about her rough life from the agency prior to this meeting.

She had lost her mother at a young age and did not go down such a good path. She had given birth to two other children (four years old and twenty months old), and the pregnancy was a surprise to all and a disappointment to others. She had planned on having an abortion. The two potential fathers had given her the money to have an abortion administered.

Some of her family members were completely against both abortion and adoption.

She had come in contact with the agency after having a dream where God told her to have this baby, but she wasn't to keep it, and she would just know the parents upon meeting them.

She mentioned how she didn't really connect with the baby like her other two. She struggled but didn't talk to this one or sing to her or grow close to her as she knew she wouldn't be keeping her.

This was hard for me to hear, but I knew in that moment that I could give her baby all those things she wasn't able to.

CHAPTER 20

Little Miracle

Joe and I visited with our birth mom for approximately two hours before she said the magical words I had been waiting to hear: "Well, I like you guys, but…"

But what? My heart sank!

Just then, a woman from the agency asked if she wanted help getting her words out. She shook her head yes, and they asked us, "She wants to know if you two"—looking at Joe and me—"would like to be the parents of her baby girl."

I looked up with tear-filled eyes and asked our birth mom, "Really? Is that what you're asking us?"

She shook her head yes as I buried my head in my lap, crying tears of joy. My heart was mending and I was beginning to not feel broken. This woman was trusting me to mother her child for her. I was overjoyed and excited for this new journey. Then Joe and I hugged each other and her. That hug lasted a good five minutes, and photos were taken as well. This moment would once more change my life forever.

When asked when the baby would be due, she answered, "In two weeks."

I had to laugh when I heard her and Joe talk about the "best" time for our baby to be born due to work schedules and all. I also had an event planned at the photo studio. It consisted of a character kids could get their photo taken with during an annual downtown festival the weekend she was due.

She had turned down three potential parents before us—one simply because of their religion. Our living situation and church attendance were very important to her. She chose us!

As we left the visitation, we thanked her for asking us to adopt her baby girl. She gave thanks for the desire within us to adopt, asking if I wanted to attend her next doctor appointment to hear the baby's heartbeat.

Of course, I wanted to hear my potential baby's heartbeat! The conversation between Joe and me during the drive home was so exciting, knowing that in two weeks, we could finally be parents!

A few days after meeting the birth mom, I stood in a doctor's office alongside her two children and a lady from the agency as the nurse prepped her belly for a heartbeat. It was the most beautiful sound I had ever heard. That thumping could be the heartbeat I could hear and love forever.

Following the appointment, we all went out for lunch. I was introduced to her kids as their "baby sister's mommy." The visit was very special as I gave each of her kids a toy. One toy included a doctor kit for her little girl. The mom had mentioned that her daughter loved playing doctor with her. Now she could play doctor with her baby sister in her mommy's belly.

I couldn't believe I was beginning to be called her mommy. During the time leading up to adopting our baby girl, we began to purchase little items here and there. We had only two weeks to prepare for our little miracle! Excitement was brewing, but we were also being very cautious since the birth mom had seventy-two hours after the child's birth to change her mind.

We bought a car seat / stroller combo but only took the car seat out of the box. We purchased a bassinet, but it stayed in the box.

While preparing for our child, we considered her name. Her birth mother liked the name *Jael* and, at one point, was planning on naming her that. She had told me that she knew her name came from the Bible but felt we should name the baby what we wanted to name her.

On Saturday (August 19, 2017), at 5:11 a.m., we received a call from a woman saying "Congratulations! You're going to be parents today!" I had to have it repeated in disbelief.

Oh my goodness! It's time! We're actually going to finally be parents!

We grabbed our previously packed bags and hung a sign at the photo studio stating that we had to cancel the event due to a "family emergency." Later, I thought the sign should have read "family blessing" instead of "emergency."

This would be the happiest early morning drive ever! Joe and I prayed and praised God together!

Upon arrival, the lady from the agency told us that the birth mom was dilated and that the baby girl would be here very soon.

I can't describe the actual feelings as it was an overwhelming love I felt from my Savior. A love so deep and strong.

He was granting me my deepest, most desirable prayer. And although the happiness filled me, so did a slight doubt—a guarding of my heart, if you will.

As Joe and I held each other outside the labor and delivery room, we still were filled with such awe. Look at God. We began to reflect over the last few years of our lives, where God had brought us from to be in this special moment. Here we were, knowing our lives would be forever positively changed. We thought about how we could experience those camping trips and Disney movies, and we would go on many more adventures with our very own child.

The woman from our agency opened the labor and delivery door to where Joe and I sat on a long wooden bench. She said, "She is now in labor and would like you to be in there with her." She was looking directly at me.

My heart may have skipped a beat at hearing those words as I was amazed. She wanted me? It was time. Time to meet our precious baby girl that God handpicked for us to parent. As we entered, Joe was asked if he wanted a chair so he could sit outside the room as no other man had been present for her other two births. The door was left slightly open so he could hear everything concerning his child's birth.

I slowly walked into the delivery room, and our birth mom and I locked eyes. I began to cry as I saw the woman carrying my baby give a look of fear. It was fear of the unknown. I had no words to comfort her.

She grabbed my hand and squeezed it so tight. There was a bond between us that only God knew the words for. She then cried out, "I'm scared."

In all honesty, so was I. What was this going to look like? Would everything go smoothly in this delivery? Would we really be taking a baby home in seventy-two hours? Many unknowns began to consume my mind. Being the giver that I am, I wanted desperately to give back to her in some way.

There was one thing I was sure of—one thing I was able to tell her right before the baby was born. I told her that we had decided on a name.

She instantly began to cry even more and asked, "Is it *Jael*?"

And I cried, shaking my head yes.

Naming her Jael was the one thing we could give to her for the special blessing she was about to give to us. I was then assisted to her feet, beside the doctor delivering our baby girl. Her birth mom knew I was a photographer, and I was granted permission to take photos during the delivery. I took two or three photos as the amazement was overwhelming. The questions continued in my brain. Did any drugs or alcohol affect the baby?

At this moment, Joe and I both heard her say, "Oh, it hurts!" And instantly, I saw a baby's head covered in straight dark hair! I had to ask the doctor if that was indeed the baby's head!

The nurse confirmed it was, and the most beautiful baby girl was now entering this world at 11:57 a.m. Once she was delivered, with the umbilical cord attached, Joe came into the room and cut the cord at the birth mom's request. She had cut her other two children's cords herself.

The look our birth mom and Joe gave each other was priceless. It was a look of amazement over the birth of this perfect child from God himself. I honestly can hardly describe what I was feeling. It was the most unreal yet beautiful sight of my life. I didn't feel worthy of this blessing. But God saw something in me that I couldn't see in myself.

CHAPTER 21

Guarded Heart

Following the birth of beautiful Jael, Joe and I were then asked to leave the room for one hour. We walked to the hospital cafeteria and met with a lady from the agency to eat lunch. Knowing the baby came out with feces on her, the doctor didn't seem too concerned. She seemed perfect, from what we could tell.

It was then that I told Joe something or someone was guarding my heart. I had also begun *to pray a different prayer. Instead of "Lord, please give me this child to mother," I prayed, "Lord, please let this be your will—110 percent your will. If we are meant to take her home with us, let it happen. If we are not meant to be her parents, as much as it will hurt, don't let it happen."*

As potential parents now, we talked about her beauty, how much hair she had, and how we were extremely excited to hold her. I had attained a cold sore the size of Texas a week prior and had to inform the nurses that I was on antibiotics for it, just to even be able to hold our baby.

After one hour, Joe and I entered a new room that they had placed the mother and baby in. It was at this time that we learned that she had breastfed her. That was great news for the first feeding nutrients, but it was also scary as we all knew it created bonding. Since I had prayed differently, God gave me an overwhelming peace that made me feel Joe and I would be fine no matter what happened.

The birth mom held the beautiful baby and then asked if we would like to hold her.

Joe held her first as he stared into his baby girl's eyes. We adored this bundled-up "little human" we called her. What a precious gift from God.

That sparkle in Joe's eyes I had only seen one other time. That was the time I was walking toward him with tunnel vision, wearing a wedding dress. He was already over the moon in love.

I instantly fell in love with this little girl as I held her so close. I observed her every finger, every toe, the little hairs on her neck and shoulders. This sweet baby girl looked at Joe and me with smiles, and such a strong connection between her and us was very apparent. How amazing.

God created the perfect little girl for us to parent. She would open only one eye and look at us as if she knew we were her parents.

Her birth mother had requested that the baby not go to the nursery alone and that we bunk in her personal room for the next three days. This was a total shock to the hospital staff as I guess this type of adoption wasn't what they had experienced in the past. This was a sweet and calm adoption, and the birth mom felt most comfortable with us in her presence.

Joe and I were assigned a room at the Ronald McDonald house and felt at home there. Every meal was provided as well as many shelves and refrigerators to choose meals from.

One day in our room, I read in my daily devotion that God was the one who was guarding my heart!

> And the peace of God, which transcends all understanding, will *guard your hearts* and your minds in Christ Jesus. (Philippians 4:7)

I told Joe, with much excitement, that I now knew WHO was guarding my heart! It was Christ!

Joe and I took turns traveling to the hospital and back to the Ronald house, even if it was only to get three hours of sleep. At the birth mom's request, we parented the baby in her room as she observed us changing diapers, feeding her, burping her, and caring for her.

It was so helpful to me as I would ask her how she did this or that with her other two children.

The birth mom and I stayed up so late every night talking about God, plans, and dreams. She made sure I was comfortable, ordering me fruit and extra pillows for my well-being. Laughter and happiness filled our hospital room.

We took turns holding the baby and talking to her, telling her about the adoption. The mother who gave birth to her loved her dearly.

This was a dream. Sometime around 5:00 a.m., Joe relieved me from the room with the baby and birth mom. He prayed with her, and at one point, she had stated that because of him, she realized not all men were so bad after all.

The baby was so loved by us all so much. The birth mom would cuddle her at times, and at other times, I would. At one point, her two children came in and met their baby sister, Joe, and me. Her birth mom asked if we thought it would be okay, and we agreed it would be good for them and, one day, the baby girl. It was precious as I took photos of them touching her tiny nose and ears, admiring her hair and fingers.

As I watched these two children adore their baby sister, I couldn't help but think of the unexplained closeness I had with them and their mother. She felt closer than a sister. Only God can explain that too.

Most of the nurses were so kind and helpful concerning the adoption. They would enter our room and stop at the door, stating that our room felt different. The birth mom and I would just smile at each other because we knew that God was the center of this adoption. We had prayed together and praised God in that room.

She breastfed that first feeding and then decided to bottle-feed, although it was a tough decision. She had breastfed her other two children. At one point, she asked my opinion of breastfeeding, and I told her to do what she felt in her heart to do. I didn't want her to have any regrets.

CHAPTER 22

Introducing Mommy

The day before the birth mom could sign the adoption papers, she asked me to do something that I wondered if I even could. As I sat in a chair holding the baby and she sat in her hospital bed, she said, "Okay, it's time. Introduce yourself to her." I asked her what she meant by this. She then said, "You haven't told the baby who you are—her mother."

I was taken aback by this as I was actually possibly becoming a mother. I responded, "I can't. You don't have to sign those papers tomorrow."

To which she said, "I need to hear it."

Wow. I was about to let that guard down. Taking a big breath in, tears sliding down my eyes, I looked deep into the precious child's eyes as the words quietly left my mouth. "Hi. I'm your mommy, and I love you."

I cried, the birth mom cried, and then the baby cried. What a beautiful moment. I imagine that since we all parented her together, the birth mom felt reassured that her baby would be cared for the way we cared for her there. It was a precious three days, parenting together this beautiful baby girl.

The time had come, and forty eight hours was upon us. As the birth mom began to pack up her room, Joe and I knew that once she left the hospital, we would still have to be there one more day with the baby. We wanted the baby to have her shots as she hadn't gotten them yet. Her mother didn't like them and chose to not receive any for the baby.

There we stood in the hospital room, the three of us: the birth mom, me, and the baby girl.

It felt very clear or light, kind of the same clear I saw when I laid the fertility burden at God's feet. The sun shone brightly in one window, illuminating the room.

The birth mom held the baby bundled in a hospital blanket and a little pink hat with a bow on it, and we cried, hugging each other.

A nurse entered the room quietly and asked to sit in the chair as she mentioned that she had never witnessed anything more beautiful in her life.

The birth mom looked up with tear-filled eyes and asked me if Joe and I would love her unconditionally and if our family would. And she asked if I promised to put big bows in her hair.

"Of course" was my response to it all as tears rolled down my cheeks.

We prayed together. We thanked God for bringing us all together. We prayed over Jael's future. This moment was so real.

She then asked the question I had no answer to. "What do I do now, just hand her to you?"

I told her to do what she knew in her heart to do. Not what I wanted. And yes, she would be loved unconditionally and taken care of in a godly home. But ultimately, this was her choice, not mine or anyone else's.

The nurse couldn't handle the emotions and, at this point, asked if she could use one of our phones to take a photo of this beautiful moment.

We kept adoring this precious gift from God in amazement. It felt like an eternity. Was everyone coming back soon to help us? Was the agency returning?

Was Joe coming back?

No. It happened just like God wanted it to. She then handed the bundled-up baby to me. We both cried, and so did the baby.

This was it. God's plan was actually happening right in front of me. How did I deserve it?

I heard her let out a loud cry as she left the room. She turned back to smile at the baby once more as she walked down the hall. It was hard for her to let her child go. She had carried this baby for nine months. A piece of her was being left in that room that day.

I had so much love and respect for this woman I had only met a few weeks prior. What a strong woman, trusting me to raise her baby. The emotions were heavy. My entire life I had the desire to be a mommy and to love and nurture one of God's special children. I knew I loved her unconditionally already but felt a sense of sadness for the woman who gave birth to my miracle. I'm sure it was hard for her to leave the baby with a woman she entrusted and only knew a few weeks prior.

CHAPTER 23

Foundation of Christ

Joe and I slept in the nursery that night. Definitely exhausted and sleep-deprived, we settled in uncomfortable chairs with nurses everywhere. We did establish a somewhat separate space to rest and care for our baby.

The next day, knowing that in the seventy-second hour, the adoption paperwork could finally be signed, we would wait.

During this time, I couldn't take my eyes off the beautiful child I cradled in my arms. Although Joe and I were very tired from little sleep, we cared for her and gleamed with happiness mixed with a little fear of the unknown. We didn't know if her birth mom would show up at a separate location to sign the adoption papers.

In the uncertainty, I adored the baby I held. So still against my chest, I couldn't tell which was my heartbeat and which one was hers. This felt so right. I touched her soft rosy cheeks and rubbed her smooth back. Every second I spent with her, I fell more in love with her. Joe and I prayed together and felt that we were right where God wanted us to be. We had faith during this time, but I couldn't rid the thoughts of sadness.

What if her birth mom chose to keep her now? Through the heartbreak, I'd have to let her go.

Joe and I didn't have much appetite or sleep but did feel the overwhelming presence of God in those long hours of waiting. God's love was so strong and sweet.

Approximately six hours later, the call came in! The birth mom had signed the papers! We were officially parents!

The joy, the happiness, the relief we both felt, like finally I could breathe again. It was definitely one of the most special moments of our lives. The baby received her shots and first bath. Shortly after, we were told we could go home with our baby girl!

That was the best news yet! I rode in the back seat with her, and at one point, I said to Joe, "Oh my gosh, honey! Do you realize that we are responsible for this little human for the rest of our lives?"

"Yes, honey," he replied.

When we arrived home, there was a poster taped to the back door, placed there by our church family. It read "Welcome home, Jael!" It came with many balloons. Later, these balloons would cause an entire block to lose power for a short time due to a metallic balloon getting wrapped into a power line. I like to say she entered our lives with a BANG!

We then walked into the house, setting the car seat and baby down in the dining room. I promised to send her birth mom a photo so she knew we made it home safely. I snapped the photo and didn't realize it until I sent it that the baby smiled so big in her sleep for that photo. Almost as if to let her birth mom know she was okay and happy.

We called our parents and let them know we were home. Joe's parents came over that night and held her, and they were just as amazed as we were. Joe, of course, had to put the bassinet together now as we needed a place for her to sleep.

Over the next few months, we had changed the spelling of her name from *Jael* to *Jaelle*. Her middle name originated from our mothers' and sisters' middle names (Ann), and her middle name (Marie) was my grandmother's—the one woman I loved so much. And I told her, if I ever had a baby girl, her middle name would be *Marie*.

So we would name her Jaelle Ann Marie.

As she grew, we could see traits from my grandma (who had passed), and it was pretty special. Just her love of life and people.

Joe and I had monthly home visits from the agency. They could tell that we loved this parent thing as we "fought" over who got "baby cuddles."

I was very blessed to attend not one but two baby showers administered for our princess. Themed pink and gray elephant, the baby showers were held in my studio. One was hosted by my immediate family, and the other was hosted by our church family. A rocking chair, big diaper cakes, books, clothes, wipes, bottles, crochet items, and many other gifts were presented to me, her mother. One gift included her dedication dress, which was created by a dear friend from my wedding dress. She even made a little handkerchief and bonnet to match. I loved dressing her up and putting big hair bows in her hair.

I began sending monthly emails as we had promised her birth mother, oftentimes attaching a few photos of her growth.

Day three of the baby's birth, this is a section of the message that was sent to the birth mom from Joe and me: *"This bond will never break as it sits on a strong foundation of Christ and love."*

A message from her birth mother to us read: *"Thank you, guys, so much for being amazing parents to her!"*

We truly felt this was a spirit-led journey that God had placed us all on together.

But something was slightly wrong in the paperwork, causing the adoption not to be final just yet. It was a minor setback for finalization. We couldn't wait for it to be final as we knew anything could happen. I believe it's fair to say Joe's faith was a little stronger here than mine. Fear crept in often with the "what-ifs."

I couldn't imagine someone taking her from me. No photos could be posted to social media, and we were to treat this somewhat like foster care. This was rough since that's what I do. I'm a photographer who likes snapping lots and lots of pictures.

CHAPTER 24

It's O-fish-al!

Jaelle began to grow so fast right before our eyes! Her biggest fan was her great-grandpa. He would cheer her on as she army-crawled across his floor and rolled over for the first time, looked upon by both great-grandparents.

She lit up every room she entered, whether it be a shopping center or a funeral.

Family loved her dearly. As Joe's parents sat and adored her, we knew they were bursting with excitement! They never thought they would have grandkids, and here was grandkid number two. Her cousin was four months old when she was born. She also had two others older than her.

Finally, we received the call that a court date was set, and about seven months from her birth, it was time to sign the papers to finalize the adoption!

Friends and family sat in court with us, and they witnessed as the judge handed her a little gavel of her own. Once again, seeing my baby's big smile was like she knew this was good. We signed our last paper through the tears, holding our miracle baby. It was FINAL! We were parents to one of God's chosen ones! A beautiful, smart, and sweet baby girl!

Joe and I hosted an adoption party titled "O-fish-ally Ours!" There were cookies, cake, balloons, and a room filled with people who loved us and her. Most of the food contained cracker goldfish and aquatic-themed snacks.

In the months to come, she began to crawl faster, and more teeth began to pop up. I tried keeping up with her baby book so she could have it one day in the future. Her baby book contains advice from her birth mother that has assisted me many times. This included moving the baby's legs like she was bike pedaling, to help her poop. Receiving parenting advice from many other mothers including my own, we enjoyed watching our baby girls growth.

She was about seven months old when Joe and I decided to have our baby dedicated to the Lord. Jaelle was dedicated at our church, and she was wearing a dress along with a bonnet all made from my wedding dress. A great friend had sewed it all just right for a little princess. Looking like an angel, we devoted our precious baby girl to the Lord surrounded by friends and family.

At her dedication, our pastor handed Joe a white carnation flower that we were to give to her on her twelfth birthday. This was to remind her of how much God loves her and explain how she was dedicated to him on this day. We placed her flower on a shelf in her bedroom, in a clear zipped bag. It would stay there for twelve years. Our baby was growing so fast right before our eyes!

On her first birthday, we had a mermaid pool party at her Nana and Papa's (Joe's parents) home.

Many of her friends and family joined her in swimming and eating cake and ice cream. Princess songs played over the speakers as we celebrated her turning a year old!

I had created a video that we watched during her party. The first slide was the sound of her heartbeat that was recorded the day I went to her doctor appointment. This was followed by the sound of her first cry as I had recorded a short video of her entering the world through delivery, which was approved by her birth mom.

It is safe to say there were many tissues being passed in the room as tears poured, watching as Jaelle was on the screen with many of the people in the room. I really tried to include everyone who attended her first birthday in her video. It was special, and we were all reminded of this blessing named Jaelle.

The next gathering quickly approached everyone. Her second party was themed "Donut Grow Up 2 Fast!" It was centered on—you guessed it—donuts! Donut pool floats and a donut bar! She had multiple photo shoots as well, as you can imagine. This was supposed to be a smaller party, but it didn't go as planned as so many friends and family joined us in celebrating Jaelle turning two!

Around this time, we thought it was time for Jaelle to get a puppy, just in case God wasn't planning a sibling. Joe and I knew we wanted a girl puppy, and through multiple phone calls, we were invited to pick out our puppy. Upon arrival, there were eight puppies in an open-top kennel, all snuggled together. One left the others and walked over to Jaelle and barked a little bark. We knew this was the one, although we had first pick of all eight! We had a puppy that Jaelle would name Anna (of course) as she was Elsa from her favorite movie, *Frozen*.

At first, she was scared of her puppy and ran from her. But that didn't last long. On week one, Jaelle had Anna in her baby stroller and was walking her around the house. Anna never put up much of a fight as she loved her human, whom she chose.

Joe and I remind her of it too. Their little bond is so cute. One thing they enjoy very much is each having a spoon of peanut butter to lick off, both on all fours. Now our family had grown to Joe and I, our little human, and our puppy, Anna.

CHAPTER 25

Roar!

Jaelle is a silly, loving, sweet, sassy, thoughtful little girl. She always considers others and their feelings. There is a funny story I must share.

One day, Jaelle was at her babysitter's, and when I arrived to pick her up, I was told that she pulled another child's hair. Jaelle saw the disappointment on my face as I had told her to be nice to her friends. Upon arriving home, I asked Jaelle, "Did you pull a little girl's hair today?"

She answered, "No, Mommy."

So I crouched down to her level and asked her a second time, and again she said no. I then asked, "Jaelle, are you telling Mommy the truth, or are you lying?"

At this question, she let out a big growling ROAR! It took me a second to realize she was pretending to be a lion. She heard the word *lying*, and she thought I said *lion*. I couldn't be serious any longer, so we began to rehearse all the animals and their sounds.

Kids have a way of making us laugh or second-guess ourselves. This silly girl brings me and her daddy so much joy. As I write now, I am still so amazed at what God has done.

I never knew a bond could be so strong between a father and a daughter or a daughter and a mother. Jaelle is our biggest, most special blessing. I remind myself of this daily, even when I'm cleaning SpaghettiOs off the wall or scooping handfuls of lotion out of her hair.

I know that one day, she will realize that she looks different from us, but I pray that we show her so much love and compassion that it doesn't matter. We trust God will continue to guide us in parenting her. She is my daughter. God answered me, and I am her mother. It's still surreal. Often, I think back to the day we saw her enter the world, and I am still just as amazed. Our baby is an absolute blessing from God.

He knew what he was doing even when I was blinded and could not see.

Looking back to when I was in my young mother's womb all the way to where God has brought me is amazing. He still works on me daily. God has changed both Joe and me to be the best "us" we can be. He has taught us that communication is number one in our marriage. We can talk about our fears or our doubts, and it's okay. We have a love for each other that I never thought I deserved. Joe loves me, and he cares about me.

This is something I struggled with my entire life due to the disappointments in my own father. Joe amazes me by how God is using him in his work and our lives. He adores Jaelle and gives her hugs and kisses daily.

We often hear of how blessed Jaelle is to have us as parents, but in reality, we are blessed to have her as our daughter. Jaelle loves family group hugs with Mommy and Daddy, and she loves tickles from us. She cuddles us both, and yes, we still "argue" over baby cuddles and who gets to hold and love on her. We will probably continue that into her adult life. She laughs and it makes us laugh. Her happiness is contagious everywhere she goes.

I love these moments of being a mommy to a little human (or toddler), and we are excited to see what her future will be! Upon decorating her room, I found a sign that read "not only is she a princess, but a warrior." This is what her birth mom said when giving birth, that Jaelle shot out of her, and she knew that Jaelle was a princess warrior. Maybe that's why, for the harvest festival at our church, Jaelle wanted to dress up as a princess warrior this year.

We still send updates and encouragement to her birth mom often as the baby girl grows. Our beautiful baby girl, at the young age of four, actually began to question me, asking, "Mommy, did I come from your belly?"

I calmly just asked her, "Well, what do you think?" I was being very careful to not say yes as we know she did not come from my belly.

So after receiving counsel from some friends and family, Joe and I decided that it was time to tell our baby the truth—her story. Oftentimes, we did what we call "bed talk." At a younger age, Jaelle would tell me stuff I couldn't understand. A year later, she began telling me how some people are mean. I plan on assisting her in "bed talk" as she grows.

We sat on her bed together. The three of us looked at one another, and as I took my baby girl's hands while staring directly in her eyes, God gave me these words: "Baby girl, you know Mommy and Daddy adore you and love you so very much, right?"

She shook her head yes.

"Okay. You know how you have been asking if you came from my belly?"

She shook her head yes once more.

"Well, sweetheart, you didn't come from my belly. You came from another woman's belly. She is called your birth mom."

At this moment, my little girl looked at peace, like she knew all along but wanted us to confirm it for her. I asked if she wanted to know her birth mother's name or see her photo again. I had put together a little book for her to keep, which contained photos of her and her birth mom. I can't say it was easy to have this conversation. I felt confident in my mothering abilities to trust God and stay calm.

I could only think that this was another miracle. I definitely wasn't expecting to have the adoption talk with her at the young age of four, that's for sure! Maybe six or seven but not four! Then I look back over the past few years. When did God ever move when I expected him to?

Never. It was always his sweet and perfect timing every time.

It was scary to talk to her, not knowing what questions it might raise in the future. It's a good thing I know who holds our future. God will be with us through every conversation, every tear, and every exciting moment. He will be there. Life sure throws us curveballs, but it's up to us how we play the game.

Shortly after this adoption conversation, Joe and I talked about moving options. We were surrounded by bars and were ready to relocate our family and puppy to a new location away from downtown. Through much prayer, we received a phone call to go look at a home about thirty minutes closer to Joe's work. It was a large Victorian-style home on a hill containing eleven acres and two ponds. I stood in amazement with the feeling of freedom.

On one visit to the home, standing in the kitchen, I shared with a friend that I had the lyrics to "Amazing Grace" framed for what would become my craft room. At that moment, she turned to a table belonging to the current homeowner. On it sat a hymnbook. A page was tabbed, and as she opened the book to it, I teared up in amazement. The song "Amazing Grace" was on that page.

I had asked God to show signs that this was the home he wanted for us, and during another visit, I saw a mommy and baby deer on the property looking at us. It is definitely a blessing God wants us to have. Of course, it needs a lot of work. With Joe and I remodeling three other homes together with the help of his workers, we knew we could make it into what we want. With wallpaper on almost every wall and ceiling, time and patience will bring a beautiful modern Victorian home for our family to enjoy in the years to come.

Joe knew someone was interested in our home, and on the same day we moved in, our place was sold as well. But God…he gave us land to enjoy with other friends and family.

Jaelle went fishing in her pond and caught a bluegill, and she joined in on a bonfire in the firepit. S'mores were a must. Some days, we enjoy doing her schoolwork on my craft room balcony (weather permitting).

Many birds are near our home, and recently, we filled up the two feeders for them. Birds were Uncle David's favorite, and since they are on my walls and windows, it's a sweet little reminder. God is now a major part of our lives, and we pray to him as a family daily.

Chapter 26

God's Incredible Love

My parents and I still struggle with communication in a healthy manner. Unfortunately it is my personal opinion, my mother is still not able to forgive herself for her actions as a young parent. I have forgiven both of my parents for any wrongdoing. We love her and pray for her often as my mother and my daughter's grandmother. Currently, I occasionally speak to my father through social media only as he still resides in and out of prison—mostly in.

My mother and I haven't had any real communication in quite some time, but I keep my faith, knowing that God will bring us close in a healthy relationship. I will always pray for healthy family relationships. I can't handle negativity in my life or my child's, and I refuse to allow my daughter to live the life I lived as she will have her own story.

I understand others may see me in a very negative light, but I also believe that God will restore those relationships in his timing and soften hearts as well. I strongly desire healthy relationships with all of my family. At times, I know it's hard for my baby girl to accept rejection. That is the same rejection I struggled with growing up. But as her mother, it is my job to keep her safe, physically and spiritually.

I'm so thankful for the relationship with my baby sister residing in Florida. Not long ago, we went to a theme park with her and my brother-in-law. It was a great visit. Boy was it fun watching my baby sister sled on our hill this winter and ride water rides with our baby girl where, of course, she got wet!

Jaelle loves everything about family and adores her Nana and Pa-paw. Her favorite activity is staying the night with them (Joe's parents). She also enjoys spending time with her cousins and having playdates often. Our baby girl also absolutely loved her great-grandpa (Joes' grandpa) and grandma as well. Last year, she had to sadly say goodbye to her great-grandma as she passed away.

Jaelle loved visiting her great-grandpa a few times a week. She calls him her best friend. When we'd visit, she would climb in his lap, and he'd gives her back rubs.

Great-grandpa began to have trouble taking care of himself, and Joe's aunt had to make the best decision for him. He had to leave his home of sixty-two years and be placed in assisted living just after turning one hundred years old! There was a big party for him as his friends and family came along with his old golf buddies. It was a great hundredth birthday party for Grandpa.

During one of our fasts with our church, we were to only watch Christian shows for a couple of weeks. Mommy, Daddy, and Jaelle watched a movie about how a mother and a son distributed five thousand blankets to the homeless. This intrigued my daughter, and she asked, "Mommy, can we make homemade Valentine's cards for the people at Grandpa's new home?"

So after only living there a few days, in came his great-granddaughter with personalized cards and candy for every resident in the assisted-living building. Grandpa sure loved every time we came to visit him. He enjoyed putting cartoons on the TV for Jaelle and receiving her snuggles as well. She made sure to always dress up for Great-grandpa in her big colorful dresses. The individuals grew to like when Jaelle would visit as she would sit and talk to them about Jesus. I was amazed as her mother to see her have a giving heart like me. Everyone in the home knew her as the little cutie who gave them a Valentine. It meant a lot to them. We got cookies for the staff.

One Tuesday, we walked into Grandpa's room as we always did on Tuesdays. Grandpa was sitting in his chair complaining of a headache, but he insisted that we stay and visit. It was a special visit where Nana came over too. Jaelle sat in Great-grandpa's lap as he rubbed her back. Before leaving, we told him we would see him on Friday of that same week. This was followed by one more huge run and a leap with a Jaelle hug!

Unfortunately, that would be her last visit with her best friend. Great-grandpa passed away peacefully a few days later as Joe was visiting and praying with him.

Telling Jaelle of his death was not easy as he was a big part of our lives. I reassured her that he was now in heaven with God and not hurting or lonely. At his funeral, she kept going over to his casket like she always did at family functions. Just making sure he was still there. At one point, she touched Grandpa's hand and told him she loved him. She also put his Valentine card containing her handprints in his casket so he could take it to heaven with him.

There were a few flowers and a blanket received by friends and family that Joe and I were told to take home. One day following the funeral, Jaelle and I opened the blanket only to read the words through tears: "Amazing grace how sweet the sound that saved a wretch like me. I once was lost but now I'm found, was blind but now I see." It was another one of God's little reminders from when my grandma died and when I was deciding a title for this book. That song came up multiple times in my decision. "Amazing Grace" and "I Once Was Blind" were a few titles I considered.

Jaelle is so smart and happy. She wanted to begin a ministry of her own once turning six years old. This would consist of her handing out free bracelets with the words "Jesus loves you" or biblical scriptures on them. Daily, when at the grocery store, the bank, or a park, she offers her bag of bracelets to everyone she came in contact with. Men, women, and children were blessed and happy to receive a free, colorful bracelet from a beautiful six-year-old. Her goal was to give one thousand bracelets before Christmas. Joe was right. Jaelle would do great things for God's kingdom. We are blessed to be parents to such an amazing little girl. We love looking at God's goodness together on car rides or at home from our porch: his clouds, his sunset, his rain, his trees, his animals, his snow, his absolute beauty. Currently, I homeschool Jaelle as Joe and I decided it was best for her in this harsh world we live in. She gets to experience so much by being homeschooled, such as a baby deer showing up in her yard.

During a visit with her God sisters, a baby deer was standing in our driveway. It then walked up to the girls. They absolutely loved it and were amazed, as was I! They hand-fed it apples and even petted the baby deer! Every day, we are amazed at God's blessings. Joe and I realize that nothing belongs to us but to God.

Without him, none of this would be possible.

The conversations of her adoption come up on a regular basis. We openly tell her the truth. Recently, she asked who was holding her in a photo she found while unpacking. Looking over, I saw the photo of her two siblings holding her in the hospital room following her birth. Back to bed talk. I explained how her birth mom wanted the best for her and realized how hard it was to raise the two children she had. She couldn't imagine raising Jaelle too. I assured Jaelle that she was so loved by them and that as she gets older, if in her heart, she desires to, she can meet them.

We don't put any holds on God. God will do what he wants to do. We just trust him along the way. A photo of her siblings holding her went into her little memory book, which she titled "Jaelle's Story." It had artwork of a stick-person Jaelle with her birth mom and siblings holding her.

Oftentimes, she comes to Mommy and Daddy's bed in the middle of the night, simply for cuddles. We snuggle and hold her close, knowing that day by day, she's growing more and more into a little princess warrior for God. We are aware that there may be a void in her heart that only God can heal. As her parents, we can be mindful of the void and simply love and shower her with God's goodness. I know, in time, God can heal that void in her heart. It's my job as her mother to always be her safe place to come to when she feels an emptiness. I make sure I let her hear me praying over her daily. I want to show her how to talk to God and to listen to his soft-spoken voice. When she does, it will be life-changing for her like it was for me.

Our special Bible verse for Jaelle is Jeremiah 29:11, which states the following:

> "For I know the plans I have for you," declares the Lord, "plans to prosper you and not harm you, plans to give you hope and a future."

I pray this book touches someone's heart. Someone who suffers addiction, rejection, or doubt. God is real. He is here.

The God I had heard about my entire life, I now truly know. I have a relationship with him, and he guides me daily. I will never return to the ways of this harsh world, and I will continue down the path that God had created for me at conception. God has blessed me so much, and now, it's my heart's desire to show the world how our Savior can turn rags to riches. My heavenly father turned my gory to his glory.

He wants us to rely on him in every part of our lives and to live God-honoring lives—lives with a purpose and a plan to spend eternity in heaven with him forever.

He has a plan for Jaelle. He has a plan for you.

My prayer right now is that God releases you from yourself.

I ask that God pours his blessings and love over what the enemy has brought to you. May he fill your every void with love, peace, and joy.

In Jesus's mighty name, amen.

No matter your story, it matters. Never compare yourself to anyone as we are created to be a blessing to others and to share our story of how God showed up.

If your story is anything like this, make today be the day you break the cycle in your life and the lives of your family members. If you have never accepted Christ, make that change right now. Get connected with fellow believers and break those chains.

To ensure you have a spot in heaven with the one who created you, with your whole heart, say this prayer:

> Lord Jesus, I come today in need of a Savior.
> I have sinned. Please forgive me. I believe you
> came to earth, and you bled and died for me.
> Come into my heart, Lord. I receive you. I desire
> a relationship with you. Help me to learn how to
> become more like you. In Jesus's name. Amen.

Well, congratulations and welcome! That is the first step. Challenges will come, but to have our Lord and Savior hold our hands through this thing called life, we can overcome any obstacle. God bless you and thank you for listening to my story.

> Amazing grace, how sweet the sound
> That saved a wretch like me.
> I once was lost, but now I'm found
> Was blind but now I see.

> The End

About the Author

Brandy is a Christian wife, a writer, and a loving home-school mom to a very special six-year-old. She also teaches Sunday school at their nondenominational church.

Her life consists of cleaning up messes around the house and hosting playdates or Bible studies throughout the week with others in the community.

It has been her dream to write a book, and with this being her first book, she looks forward to writing more and continues to encourage others. This new journey is an exciting one where God gets all the glory.

Brandy resides in the Ohio area with her husband and daughter.

Printed in the USA
CPSIA information can be obtained
at www.ICGtesting.com
CBHW031819261024
16400CB00037B/472